THE OWNERS of MELBOURNE HALL

Howard Usher

ISBN 0 946404 22 4

Typeset by Howard Usher

Printed and Published by
J. H. HALL & SONS LIMITED
Siddals Road, Derby DE1 2PZ
Tel: Derby (0332) 45218 Fax: (0332) 296146

THE DERBYSHIRE HERITAGE SERIES

Introduction

When King Henry I created the Bishopric of Carlisle in 1133, he endowed it with the Rectories of Melbourne and Chellaston and the Manor of Barrow-upon-Trent. We have no knowledge of a Rectory House of this period, although it has been suggested that the so-called "Tithe Barn", which has the style of a medieval upper-floor hall and undercroft could incorporate the shell of such a building. Because of its remoteness from Melbourne and the problems of collecting the tithes due, the Bishop of Carlisle leased the Rectory to laymen from 1530. In 1592, the Rectory was leased by Sir Francis Needham, who complained that the Rectory House was in exceedingly great decay, and set to work to make it habitable. This is presumably, the forerunner, on the same site, of Melbourne Hall. He set to work to make the house habitable, and this was the building which confronted Sir John Coke when he purchased the lease of the Rectory in 1628.

This booklet contains short biographies of the lives of the owners of Melbourne Hall from Sir John Coke, through eleven generations to the present owner, Lord Ralph Kerr. Although the descent is in a direct line, there are four changes of surname, from Coke to Lamb to Cowper to Kerr, because of descent by the female line. The extensive muniment at Melbourne has been drawn upon for much of the information presented, although national history books have been used for background detail of those owners who were involved in national affairs.

Until 1752, the New Year started on the 25th March (old style) after which the modern system with the year starting on the 1st January was introduced (new style). In order to avoid confusion, all year dates have been converted to the modern system.

The illustrations are from photographs in the possession of Melbourne Hall or the author. Photographs of Melbourne Hall portraits were taken by Mr. Thomas Tivey of Melbourne. The sketch of Beauvale House was drawn by Mr. Jack Bronson of Eastwood.

I am grateful to Jill Weston, curator at Melbourne Hall and Michael Morris of J.H.Hall & Sons Ltd. for suggesting the topic and scope of this booklet; to Lord Ralph Kerr for permission to use the extensive Melbourne Hall archive, upon which this booklet is based and to my wife, Lindsay, for reading the proofs and correcting my grammar.

Howard Usher
Melbourne
1993.

The Owners of Melbourne Hall

Sir John Coke, Kt.	1563-1644
Sir John Coke the Younger, Kt.	1608-1650
Thomas Coke,	1609-1656
Colonel John Coke,	1653-1691
Vice-Chamberlain Thomas Coke,	1675-1727
George Lewis Coke,	1715-1750
Sir Matthew Lamb, Bt.,	1704-1768
Peniston Lamb, 1st Lord Melbourne,	1748-1828
William Lamb, 2nd Lord Melbourne,	1779-1848
Frederic Lamb, 3rd Lord Melbourne,	1782-1853
Emily Lamb, Lady Palmerston,	1787-1869
Francis de Grey, 7th Earl Cowper,	1834-1905
Lady Amabel Kerr,	1846-1906
Lord Walter Kerr,	1839-1927
Captain Andrew Kerr,	1881-1929
Peter Kerr, 12th Marquis of Lothian,	1922-
Lord Ralph Kerr,	1958-

"Melbourne Hall was, and mercifully is, one of the most exquisite of the smaller stately homes of England, while the formal gardens ....are as close to perfection as any in the country..."

Philip Ziegler

Sir John Coke, 1563-1644.

Sir John Coke was born in London on 5th March, 1563, the second son of Richard Coke of Trusley in Derbyshire. Trusley is about 5 miles west of Derby and John Coke looked on Trusley as his home. His father, Richard Coke, sold the residue of his ancestor's lands in Marchington, Egginton and Oslaston, and bought property in Trusley and Pinxton. John's elder brother, Francis, inherited this property on the death of their father in 1582, leaving John to make his own way in life with an annuity of £40 a year. John graduated in 1584 with an M.A. at Trinity College, Cambridge, where he remained several years as a Fellow.

He entered the service of Lord Burghley, Queen Elizabeth's Secretary of State, where he became friendly with Fulke Greville, the son of the Earl of Warwick. A later writer recalled the time when "upon Lord Brooke's entreaty, you left Trinity College in Cambridge to travail for your country's service". John Coke lodged with Greville in Essex House in the Strand. Greville employed Coke to collect information for him in Europe and between 1593 and 1597, Coke travelled extensively on the Continent. Correspondence reveals that he spent some time in Frankfurt, Heidelberg, Hungary, Sienna, Venice and Paris. In 1598, Greville was appointed Treasurer of the Navy with Coke as his Deputy Treasurer. Coke took the responsibility of financing the provisioning and manning of the ships of the Queen's Navy, which were engaged in expeditions against Spain, Ireland, and France.

In 1603, Queen Elizabeth died and James VI of Scotland was proclaimed James I of England. Coke was now 40 years old and unmarried but had started courting Mistress Mary Powell of Preston Court, Much Marcle, Herefordshire. He asked his brother, Francis Coke of Trusley, to find a suitable estate in Derbyshire for him to purchase. Francis wrote that Sharrow Hall, where Thomas Gregson dwelt, in Thurveston, Sutton-on-the-Hill was available for letting at 100 marks a year. It had on it a very pretty house with a dovecot. In 1604, John Coke decided to resign from his position at Court and take up farming in the county of Herefordshire, where Mary Powell lived. He married her the same year.

In 1606, he purchased Hale Court in Much Marcle, demolished the old house and built a new one which was ready for occupation in 1608. A son, Joseph, was born in 1605, followed by John in 1608, then Thomas, Mary, Elizabeth and Anne. It may have been at this time that he took an interest in the theatre as shown by a fragment of the rough manuscript for a play found in the Melbourne Muniments. The author is unknown but it has been attributed to John Webster, a contemporary of Shakespeare. A crude sketch of a circular London playhouse accompanied the fragment.

Coke's friend, Fulke Greville, was also a poet and dramatist. For many years, Coke farmed his Herefordshire estate, but eventually, the bright lights of London beckoned. He had never lost contact with his old friend, Fulke Greville, and had assisted Greville in the running of his estates. By 1614, Greville was appointed Chancellor of the Exchequer and called Coke up to London, where he persuaded him to stand as a Member in the 1614 Parliament.

Coke was now diverted from his intention to become a country gentleman and in 1618, he was appointed Commissioner for the Navy under the Lord High Admiral, the Duke of Buckingham. Three years later, he was elected a Member of Parliament for Greville's Borough of Warwick and in the following year, he was appointed Master of Requests to the King. In this position, he had to deal with the hundreds of petitions on all manner of subjects, which were made to the King. Examples of such petitions are the request of the Yeomen of the Guard for a wage increase, the petition of Richard Chambers, a prisoner in the Fleet, for speaking two words for which "hee is hartily sorry hee spooke them" and that of the fishermen of Barking (over 500 of them) for a patent for an engine called a trawl for catching fish. Sir John moved his household to the Gate House in St. John's, near Smithfield, and, in 1623, he moved to Austin Friars "against the Dutch church door" and never returned to Herefordshire. An account for Hale Court is entitled "1623 July 19, being the day of our removal from Hale Court". Later, he moved to the Black House, Tottenham, to escape the plague and finally settled at Garlick Hythe, near Bow Lane, which was to be his London home for many years.

1624 was a very mixed year for John Coke. In January, his eldest son, Joseph, died of smallpox whilst at Trinity College, Cambridge. In February, Coke was elected Member of Parliament for St. Germans in Cornwall and in March his wife, Marie, died at the birth of their seventh child, Dorothy. In September, he was knighted by King James, and in November, he married Joan Gore, the daughter of Sir John Lee and widow of an Alderman of the City of London.

Sir John Coke received a letter on 25 March,1625, which showed concern at the state of King James. "The King slept this afternoon from one or two o'clock till five and then waked being in a great sweat, and as they feared falling into his fit..." James died soon afterwards and his son, Charles, was proclaimed King. Sir John Coke was confirmed in his positions of Master of Requests and a Commissioner of the Royal Navy.

In September, 1625, Coke was summoned to Plymouth by the King, who was engaged in fitting out a fleet to sail on Cadiz. Here Sir John was appointed a Privy Councillor and Principal Secretary to King Charles.

The Cadiz expedition was a failure, partially owing to the inability of the men to capture a bridge owing to "their great disorder with wine". Spanish ships from Dunkirk continued to harry the Kent and East Anglian coasts. Sir John then made the first of his land purchases: that of the estate of Baggrave in Leicestershire, valued at £8,000. This estate had been depopulated by the Abbot of Leicester in the 15th century and consisted only of a sheep ranch with Baggrave Hall and the responsiblity for part of Hungarton church.

1628 found Sir John Coke in Portsmouth, supervising the fitting out of a fleet to relieve the Spanish blockade of the port of La Rochelle, whose inhabitants were in dire extremity. But Sir John's thoughts lay in another direction. He was now 64 years old, a comparatively rich man, and had been looking for a retirement home in Derbyshire for some time. His brother, Francis Coke of Trusley, had told him that Sir Francis Needham intended to sell the Rectory of Melbourne with Chellaston and the manor of Barrow-upon-Trent, which was leased from the Bishop of Carlisle. Included in the sale was the freehold estate of Melbourne Park, an ancient hunting park of the Dukes of Lancaster, purchased by Needham from the Crown in 1597. In June of 1628, Sir John paid his deposit of £600 and went to inspect the estate. It was all that he was looking for and he soon clinched the bargain for £6,600.

The rectory house had been described by Sir Francis Needham as in "exceeding great decay" and he had attempted to make it habitable, but Sir John realised that a major rebuilding was essential. In addition to his work at court, he found time to produce a 32 page specification for the rebuilding of Melbourne Hall. This contained the instructions to the masons, carpenters, tilers, smiths, glaziers and plumbers and the result of this work can be recognised in the present kitchen, dining room and study at Melbourne. The stone was taken from the foundations of Melbourne Castle which had been purchased and demolished by the Earl of Huntingdon in 1604 and some stone was brought from Hartshorne. The roofing slates came from Swithland. The work was carried out during 1630 and 1631 and cost about £600.

Sir John had other problems with his Melbourne purchase. By 1632, the Lord of the Manor of Melbourne, who was the Earl of Huntingdon, had come to an agreement with the freeholders to create a partial enclosure of the open fields. All he needed was Sir John Coke's agreement. Sir John's brother, Francis, thought it would be beneficial to Sir John, but added "how it will be good for the poor, when the commons are taken away, I yet see not". He recommended his brother to take care in settling his estate, for the freeholders were "a multitude of stubborn people and with forbearance, they are made worse".

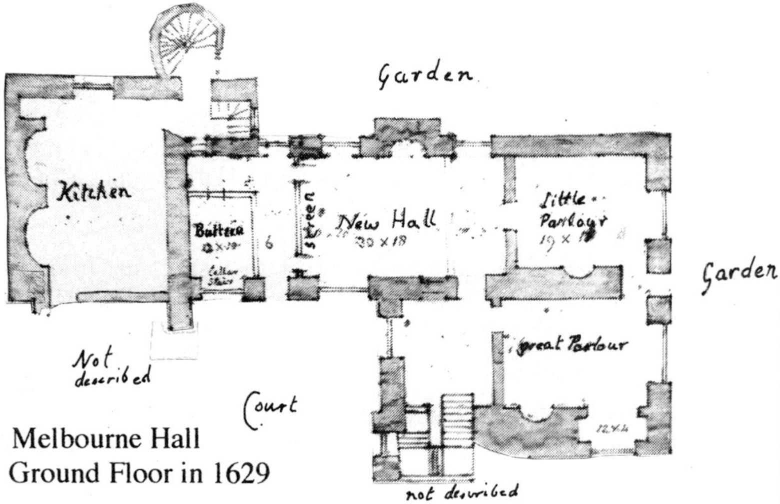

Melbourne Hall
Ground Floor in 1629

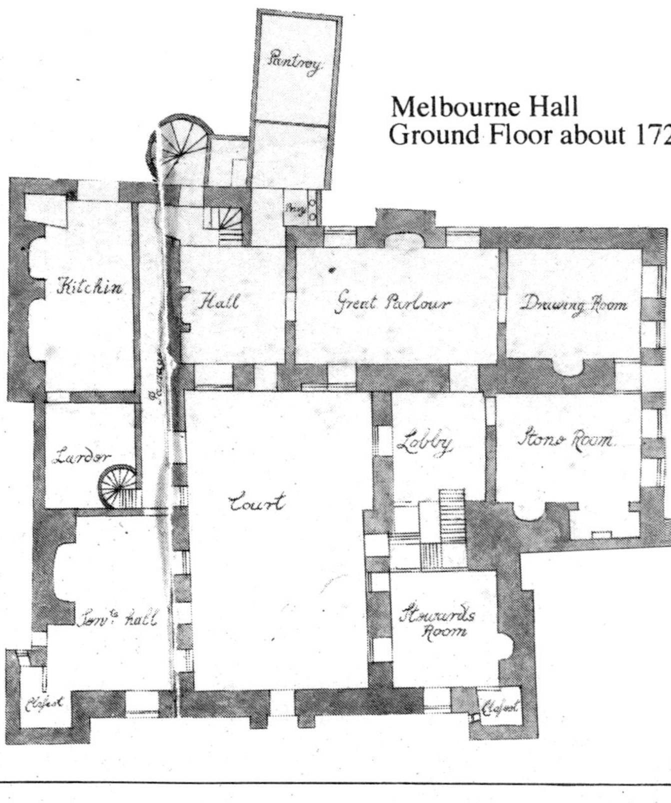

Melbourne Hall
Ground Floor about 1720

The Dining Room at Melbourne Hall

Sir John visited Melbourne in 1628 to view his purchase and again in the summer of 1630 when construction was under way. His next visit seems to have been in 1633, on his way back from accompanying the King on his 72-day progress through Scotland. The following year, his books were sent to Melbourne and the house was now ready for his retirement. His son, John, took up residence there to run the estates.

In May, 1631, Sir John purchased the Derbyshire Manor of Winlands and Over Haddon Hall and demesne for £4,500. This gave him property in Over Haddon, Bakewell, Chelmorton and Monyash. The Manor of Ashbourne was purchased the same year. In 1633, the Manor of Castle Donington was purchased for the sum of £1,398.1s.10½d. Sir John had had several clashes with the Earl of Huntingdon, who lived at Donington Park and was Lord of the Manor of Melbourne. As Sir John was now Lord of the Manor of Castle Donington, the Earl of Huntingdon had to pay a chief rent to Sir John for Donington Hall and Park.

In July, 1634, Sir John Coke wrote to the Earl of Newcastle at Welbeck Abbey, warning him that "a great multitude of miners assemble themselves at Baslow with purpose to come tomorrow morning to your house to present a mutinous petition, which is not sufferable in a well-governed state..." The lead miners were complaining about the tithe which was levied by the clergy on their lead ore production. At Chesterfield, a proclamation was read out, commanding all the miners to depart. The miners' petition was delivered, but several hundred miners headed for Nottingham and a number of the ringleaders were arrested and put in Derby gaol. However, in October, the Countess of Devonshire petitioned for their release and the minor rebellion faded away.

Although now over seventy years of age, Sir John did not let go of his position as Principal Secretary of State. He was responsible for organising the drainage of the Fens with Vermuyden and for the introduction of the hated Ship Tax in 1635. On July 5, 1636, King Charles issued an instruction to the Lord Deputy of Ireland to make a grant to Sir John Coke "in consideration of his good and faithful service to us and our Crown" of the manor of Castle Kevyn and the territory of the Fairtree in County Wicklow. The property had been confiscated by the Crown in 1596 after a Catholic uprising, but it was of little use to Sir John as it was lost sight of in another rebellion in Ireland in 1641. It is probable that the King considered this grant to be a "golden handshake", but if so, Sir John did not take the hint and did not proffer his resignation.

The King's attempts to impose the Anglican religion on Scotland resulted in the formation of an army of Scottish Covenanters who were threatening Carlisle, Hexham and Berwick. In April of 1639, Charles gathered an army and marched up to Berwick to meet the Covenanters. Sir John Coke accompanied him on this gruelling expedition. In May, the King set up his camp $2^1/_2$ miles west of Berwick on the river Tweed, where he arranged terms with the Covenanters who said that "we desire nothing but the preservation of our religion and laws." There were celebrations and bonfires in London at the news of the peace and the King was able to leave Berwick. Sir John stopped off at Melbourne on his way home and spent the whole of the month of August, 1639, at his house. On September 4th, his secretary wrote: "Your Honour's return is so much desired and expected that His Majesty doth now daily inquire after your coming".

Coke returned to London, but it was now obvious that the King required his resignation and it was with a bad grace that, in January, 1640, Coke accepted the inevitable. He wrote to his son, John, at Melbourne: "I know you have heard of the resolution taken for my retreat from Court, yet I find both a gracious countenance and profession that no offence is taken against me.....I shall now bring upon you a great family to pester your house, but not to charge your purse..." His daughter-in-law, Elizabeth, responded: "...I cannot but account it a blessing of quiet and rest to yourself, and of great happiness and contentment to us, you having resolved to entertain your time hereafter with us here in the country..." Sir John Tonstall wrote from Whitehall: "...I cannot but let you know that there are many good men here that are heartily sorry that you are not in place to do His Majesty that service which now cannot so well be done..."

Sir John Coke was now 76 years old and should have welcomed the rest at Melbourne, but the times were bad and he was not destined for a peaceful retirement. In May he wrote to the Earl of Holland "I live at home in silence and in peace, I thank God, and meddle with no business but what concerns my private..." He lamented the breakdown of law and order, quoting violence and outrage by soldiers against the inhabitants of Breedon as they left divine service. His son had enclosed his property at Derby Hills, which was a part of the Manor of Castle Donington, to prevent trespassing by the inhabitants of Ticknall and Calke. This caused a riot in June, 1640, when Sir John Beaumont's army were hired and encouraged by Sir John Harpur and the people of Ticknall and Calke to pull up the rails about Derby Hills and to set fire to the mill there.

Sir John Coke the younger had been elected Knight of the Shire of Derby and his brother, Thomas, was also in Parliament as the member for Leicester. As the tragic set of circumstances and misunderstandings led to the inevitable Civil War, both sons wrote frequent letters to their father at Melbourne describing the turbulent and momentous events which occurred in Parliament between 1640 and 1642. The atmosphere was such that many of these letters are unsigned and occasionally written in a disguised hand. As son John wrote: "Everybody had need be careful what they write for fear of interception". At another time, he wrote: "Whether this shall ever come to your hands, I know not." Sir John's brother, George, the Bishop of Hereford, was imprisoned in the Tower for 17 weeks, along with a number of other Bishops. Sir John himself was ambivalent about which side he supported; he just wanted to be left alone.

The situation polarised when Charles raised his standard at Nottingham on 22nd August, 1642. The Earl of Lindsey wrote to Coke to supply any arms he had for His Majesty and a similar letter was received from Sir George Gresley and Sir John Gell on behalf of Parliament. In the event, it was Peter Knyveton who collected 8 muskets, 2 bandoleers and 8 pikes for His Majesty's use. Sir John's horses were taken by Parliament, but were returned to him after the intercession of his son who claimed his father's "affections unto and forwardness in the service of Parliament".

At the beginning of 1643, Major Swallow's troop was billeted in Melbourne Hall. The Parliamentary commander, Sir William Brereton, took care to preserve the Hall from the disorders of the soldiers. Nevertheless, the situation was intolerable to Sir John and, in spite of the winter season, he moved to the house of his daughter, Elizabeth Danvers at Swithland for a few days. It was at this time that Richard Baxter, the Puritan minister from Kidderminster, came to Melbourne Hall, suffering from cold and severe nose-bleeding. His physicians thought that he was dying and as he contemplated death, the idea for his book "The Saints' Everlasting Rest" came into his mind.

Sir John travelled on to his wife's home in Tottenham to appeal against his levy and stayed there for several months before returning to Melbourne with a pass from his son in August of 1643. However the situation in Melbourne was no better and in November, he again asked his daughter, Elizabeth, if she could accommodate him at Swithland. She explained that the family had left Swithland and were living in Leicester where they had four families sharing the house. It was possible that she could find him a quiet place in Leicester.

In January of 1644, Sir John Coke wrote to his son, John: "You will hear by others how we have been used at Melbourne, which though at first I resented very much for your privilege of parliament....I resolved to bear all with patience, since, first by Gell's and now by Newcastle's forces, I have lost all I had in this country, and have no more here to lose where I had above 400£ a year..." At the age of 81, Coke had to uproot himself again and travel to his wife's home at Tottenham where he died on 8 September, 1644, Sir John Coke has been called "The Last Elizabethan". Certainly, his courteous and civil manner were out of place in the England of the 1640's. He has been accused of being subservient to the King and this may well be true: in this period, it was the only means of a long life. But when Charles was in trouble and trying to save his kingdom, Sir John was not there to help with words of wisdom and caution.

Sir John Coke in his robes
as Master of Requests.
(about 1622)
Portrait by
Cornelius Jannsens.

Sir John Coke the Younger, 1608-1650.

The second son of Sir John Coke, he was born in 1608 and like his father and his elder brother, Joseph, he went to Trinity College, Cambridge. Joseph died in 1624 and John then became the heir to his father's estates. His tutor described his behaviour as "civil and studious", although he would travel from London on horseback, when instructed to go by coach. This was "partly by reason of the tedious and wearisomeness of the passage, sitting from 5 in the morning till almost nine at night, plunging in the cold and dirt and dark, and that for two whole days with strange company".

In 1632, he started courting Elizabeth, the daughter of Timothy Pusey of Selston and the widow of William Willoughby, who had died a few years earlier. Elizabeth's father-in-law thought that he had never met a more intellectual young gentleman, but Elizabeth's love was so cold that he couldn't give any hope of success. In 1633, the young John was knighted and this may have changed Elizabeth's mind. Timothy Pusey wrote to Sir John that his daughter was inclined to affect young John: "Your noble son's sweet conditions hath drawn all our affections to him". They were married at Selston on 25th July,1633, and took up residence at Melbourne Hall.

The young Sir John was put in charge of the Melbourne estates and he started to view them and reported back to his father. He found that the copyholders at Castle Donington and Ashbourne had not held proper manor courts for years and were resistant to any change. He reported on the conditions of the woodlands and the mills in the estate and decided that he needed an able and honest steward to run it. He concluded that his father would "find Melburne a seate worthie to bee esteemed both for pleasure and profitt". The newlyweds visited Uncle George Coke, the Bishop of Bristol, and spent some time in Bath, where George wrily commented: "They are gone in health much like in which they came, but certainly in purse much lighter". Young John was fond of hawking and his father occasionally made him presents of tiercels and peregrines.

In 1639, the elder Sir John was interested in purchasing the manor and rectory of Duston, near Northampton, from Sir Fulke Greville. This estate had been part of the dissolved monastery of St. James and included the site of Northampton Castle. Young Sir John made a survey of the manor and found that "you shall be bounde to uphould the ruinous old walls of the castle, for it is allmost impossible to keepe them standing, the force of the mortar being eaten out with age." The negotiations were not completed until 1645, by which time Sir John the elder was dead.

When his father retired to Melbourne in 1640, Sir John the younger was able to pick up his own life. He was elected Knight of the Shire for Derbyshire in November, 1640, and took his seat in what was to be known as "The Long Parliament". His election expenses for the entertainment and lodging of his supporting freeholders came to £193.1.8. He immediately entered a Parliament seething with intrigue, which impeached Charles's Lieutenant-General, the Earl of Strafford, for treason in his dealings with the Scots. Sir John the younger was absent from the vote which declared Strafford a traitor, and his father chided him for deserting his religion and his country. He replied: "My absence from the vote I hope hath not deserved so severe a censure as is laid upon me by some...I was casually away that evening, not expecting that vote in the afternoon." The long letters he wrote to his father detailing the happenings in that eventful Parliament have already been mentioned.

He assisted a Parliamentary transfer of arms from Hull to Chester in 1642 by providing his Wilne ferry boats to transport the arms from Nottingham to King's Mills in Castle Donington, and thence he provided carts and horses to transfer them to Swarkestone and through Derbyshire. The King censured the Earl of Devonshire, threatening imprisonment in the Tower when he was caught. In the summer of 1642, Sir John observed that every street was full of soldiers, but "My prayers are for peace, and that it may not come anywhere to blows". He was appointed a Commissioner for Derby, along with Sir John Curzon, Sir John Gell, Sir George Gresley and Mr.Burdett, to receive subscriptions of money, plate and horse to the Parliament.

In January, 1643, Edward Reed wrote to Sir John Coke the elder: "The return of Sir John Coke is welcome to many in the House of Commons, where he hath gained much love and respect for his wise and temperate carriage". After much heart searching, Sir John the younger took the new Oath and Protestation and entered into the Solemn League and Covenant. Surprisingly, for these difficult times, he was still able to record that he was able to collect the rents from Baggrave.

After the Battle of Naseby, King Charles escaped to Newcastle where he was taken by the Scots. In February, 1647, Parliament managed to pay off the Scots army and in return, were allowed to have the King back. Sir John Coke was one of the nine Commissioners who rode to Newcastle to collect Charles and take him to Holdenby House, where he was kept under guard. In November, Charles escaped and fled to Carisbrooke Castle in the Isle of Wight where he attempted to obtain assistance to create Royalist uprisings.

After the trauma of the Civil War, Sir John was able to relax a little in Melbourne Hall, the house rebuilt by his father. He realised that the tiny garden attached to the house was inadequate and came to an agreement with the freeholders to close a public road that ran along the east side. This allowed the expansion of the gardens to the east and Sir John built two fish ponds or "moats" in his extension.

On 30 March, 1648, Sir John appointed his brother, Thomas, his attorney, during his absence "with the licence of His Majesty and the Parliament intending speedily to travell to the partes beyond the seas". The reason for his journey is not known, but he never returned to England. The trial and execution of King Charles took place in January, 1649, and Sir John Coke died childless in Paris in 1650, and was buried in London.

Thomas Coke, c.1609-1656.

As the third son of Sir John Coke the elder, Thomas did not expect to inherit the Melbourne estates, but circumstances decided otherwise and presented him with some difficult problems. He followed his father and his two brothers to Trinity College, Cambridge, where he studied law. He then set up in business in chambers at Grays Inn. In 1633, he invited his brother, John, to Grays Inn for Christmas as King Charles had requested that the several Inns of Court should provide him with a masque at Court at Christmas. Even in October, there was no law studied there as all the Inns had turned into dancing schools but Thomas was afraid that Grays Inn would give a weak performance.

In 1640, Thomas was selected as Member of Parliament for the Burgesses of Leicester Borough, and joined his brother, John, in the Long Parliament. He wrote to his father to inform him that the Donington copyholders had a suit in the King's Bench to stay the payment of their fines to Sir John. In May, 1640, he reported on a great multitude of about 800 people, who assaulted the Archbishop of Canterbury's house at Lambeth but the Archbishop was able to escape in a boat over to Whitehall. In 1641, John Pym, the leader of the House of Commons, wished to punish a constable who had disobeyed a Commons order for the deposing of images in churches. Thomas Coke opposed this and said that by law, the House could not inflict a punishment. He won the debate, but from then on, he was a marked man as a "malignant" supporter of the King

Thomas was taken ill at Christmas, 1641, and wrote to his father explaining that he would be unable to visit Melbourne at Christmas. He had been to visit his Uncle George, the Bishop of Hereford, in the Tower.

"Here hath been the saddest and most tumultuous Christmas that in all my life I ever yet knew." Thousands of citizens had been rioting in London and offering affronts to the Bishops and the King, and there had been clashes with the soldiers. "I fear God hath some heavy judgment to inflict upon this nation." The Inns of Court went to Whitehall to testify to their affection for the King and tendered him their services. However, it seems that Sir John Coke, the elder, disagreed with his son and the letters stop after March, 1642.

Thomas continued to speak his mind in Parliament and in January, 1645, he was voted "incapable of sitting". In September, he was expelled from Parliament for "being in the King's quarters and adhering to that party". In 1648, an ordinance was passed for pardoning his delinquency on payment of a fine of £500. By this time, brother John had left England and had given Thomas power of attorney over his Melbourne estates. When news came that John was dead and Thomas had inherited the estates, he was apprehended and brought before the Council of State as a traitor. He escaped but was captured and put into Newgate gaol. He was then ordered to leave town and to be of good behaviour but was allowed to return to London to bury his brother in August.

A curious condition was applied to Thomas's inheritance. The Melbourne estates were put into a Trust and could only revert to Thomas upon his marriage with any woman except Jane, the daughter of William Littleton of Stretton, Salop. It is not clear whether this condition was applied by Sir John Coke or by the Commonwealth, perhaps it was the latter. Thomas then married Mary Pope of Woolstaston, Salop and was able to claim his inheritance. A son, John, was born on St.Thomas's Day, 1653. But Thomas had not finished with Jane Littleton. In April, 1654 a command was issued by the Lord Protector to bring Jane Littleton before the Sessions to answer the complaint of Thomas Coke. What this complaint was we do not know, but it was settled by Thomas agreeing to pay Jane a total of £200 spread over four years.

An order for Compounding was issued by the Commonwealth which required all Royalists to pay a fine equal to the tenth part of their estates. In Thomas's case, this came to £2,200. Thomas's property in Melbourne, Ashbourne, Over Haddon, Duston and Castle Donington had been seized and granted to various owners over the previous few years but he was able to recover much of it and paid a first instalment of £1,100 in September, 1650. He was then able to retire to Melbourne for a quiet life, disturbed only by a fire at Melbourne House in February, 1656. It is assumed that he died at Melbourne and was buried in the church on the 23rd December,1656. His widow, Mary, paid £20 to Mr.Allen, the herald painter, for 30 buckram escutcheons, 2 great arms, 6 bosses for the horse's foreheads, a velvet pallet and coach hire for Thomas's funeral.

Mary did not long survive her husband and was buried beside him in Melbourne church on 27 March, 1657.

Colonel John Coke, 1653-1691.

John Coke was born on St.Thomas's Day, (perhaps 21st December), 1653, and was orphaned before his fourth birthday. As the heir to considerable property, he was made a ward of court and was put under the guardianship of Richard Pope, a relative of his mother's. The estates were run by the steward, John Radcliffe, who was accountable to Pope. It seems that Melbourne Hall was leased to tenants; in 1662, it was occupied by Richard Ford who paid a tax on 14 hearths. About this time, Sir Francis Burdett of Foremark became John Coke's guardian and was responsible for the custody of his person and his education. It seems probable that young John spent some time at Foremark while Sir Francis was building Foremark Church. Later guardians included Edward Litherland and Gilbert, Lord Archbishop of Canterbury.

His guardians were successful at building up John Coke's property and seem to have invested his profits wisely. The Honor and Manor of Melton Mowbray were purchased in 1668 and the Rivett estate in Kings Newton in 1671. In 1672, Swanick's farm at Oswestry was bought.

On the 15th June, 1670, with the approval of his guardian, John Coke married Mary Leventhorpe in the parish church of Sawbridgeworth, Hertfordshire. Mary was the heiress to Sir Thomas Leventhorpe of Shingle Hall who owned property in Hertfordshire and Essex.

John Coke became of age in 1674 and recovered his father's chambers in Grays Inn which had been lost in the Civil War and, after a long struggle, recovered his grandfather's Irish estate in County Wicklow, where he built a Protestant church at Dillossery. In 1678, he bought Blakesware Hall with its estate in Hertfordshire for £5,600 in silver. In July, 1679, his father-in-law visited Melbourne but was killed by a kick from a horse at Elvaston, and his property all devolved upon John Coke. This included the mansion house of Shingle Hall with property at Thorley, Sawbridgeworth and Ugley. In 1686, he purchased a farm at Ticknall, in 1688 some land at Breaston and, in 1690, a farm at Wilson.

John and Mary had seven children. The eldest, Thomas, was born in 1675 and he was followed by Elizabeth ("Betty"), Mary, Alice, John, Dorothy and Francis. Dorothy and Francis both died in infancy. Worn out with all this child-bearing, John's wife, Mary, died in January, 1682, and was buried in Melbourne church. In 1679, Jacob Huysmans had been commissioned to paint a portrait of John Coke's children. The portrait shows Thomas, Alice, Betty, Mary and John, playing at shepherds with Dorothy, who died at the age of 6 weeks, as an angel watching them. The portrait with frame cost £68.7.0. and hangs above the staircase in Melbourne Hall.

John Coke's Family. Portrait by J.Huysmans.

Coke was not content with just being a prosperous gentleman of property and wished to make his presence known on the national scene. He stood as a candidate for Leicestershire in the 1679 election where he was defeated by Sir John Hartop by 2,235 votes to Coke's 1,995 votes. He claimed the invalidity of the result as Sir John had 50 false names and 331 "no votes". In November, 1684, John Coke was admitted as Gentleman Usher of the Privy Chamber in ordinary to H.M.the Queen. He was successful in the 1685 and 1689 elections when he was elected to represent the Borough of Derby in Parliament. In March,1685, he was appointed Deputy-Lieutenant of Derbyshire, but he was sufficiently unwise to comment unfavourably on a statement of King James II respecting Popish recusants in November of that year. For this, he was committed to the Tower of London, and this event may have hardened his support for the Protestant cause.

Under the guise of religious toleration, King James II was accused of introducing creeping Catholicism. This did not matter as long as his Protestant Whig daughter, Mary, was heir to the throne, but when the King's second wife, who was a Catholic, produced a son in 1688, the English Protestants became alarmed. A number of nobleman, including the Earl of Devonshire, invited Mary with her husband, William, Prince of Orange, to come to England to claim the throne. John Coke supported this ideal and raised a troop of horse in the regiment of the Earl of Devonshire in the summer of 1688.

When William and Mary landed at Brixham on 5th November, 1688, Captain John Coke mobilised his troop who marched to Derby, Mansfield and Nottingham as shown by the accounts produced by his Quartermaster, Deprepetit. His cousin, Richard Pope, was cornet (an officer cadet) and carried John Coke's colours. More than three thousand men had moved to Nottingham out of Cheshire and Lancashire and Coke observed: "..all the counties around are in a flame...They declare for a free Parliament: what they desire to do I know not...." The reason soon became clear when it was seen that King James's younger daughter, the Princess Anne, had fled from London to Nottingham under the protection of the Earl of Devonshire. On 26 November, William of Orange ordered Princess Anne to join him at Oxford and the Earl of Devonshire's regiment with John Coke's troop escorted her there. Deprepetit's accounts show that they went via Leicester, Harborough, Northampton, Towcester (where they needed a guide), Banbury and Woodstock to Oxford. On 22 December, two troops were disbanded and paid off by John Coke. Deprepetit noted that his 110 men were quarrelling but they had all been paid and were "resolved to follow you wherever you will be pleased to lead them." Most other soldiers had not been paid and all regiments came to Deprepetit for money: "I have still the two bags full which I brought from Melbourne."

John Coke went on to London, while his troop returned to Derby. On 23 December, James II had effectively abdicated by fleeing to France and William and Mary had entered London. On 31 December, 1688, William, Prince of Orange, appointed Captain John Coke as Lieutenant-Colonel of the Regiment of Horse, whose Colonel was William, Lord Cavendish. An election was held in January, 1689, for which Colonel John Coke, was elected as Member for the Borough of Derby, in what became known as the Convention Parliament. On 25 February, 1689, Lord Cavendish, Colonel of His Majesty's Regiment of Horse, was ordered to repair to quarters.

However, there was still unrest in the country and John Coke's troop of 45 horsemen were ordered to Newark. There was a skirmish with the King's Regiment of Dragoons at Folkingham, near Sleaford, and they then rode to Doncaster, York and Newcastle. Charles Fitzwilliam wrote to Coke about a mob at Newcastle who had pulled down the statue of the late King James in the market place. The troops were not involved and remained quietly in their quarters. But John Coke had suffered "a dangerous indisposition" and by August, 1689, he resigned his troop which was taken over by Colonel Charles Fitzwilliam. Nevertheless, the King renewed his Commission in July,1690.

To recuperate from his illness, John Coke went to Europe where he travelled extensively. In June,1691, he left Rome for a tour of Italian cities: Sienna, Leghorn, Genoa, Florence and Bologna. He then went to Innsbruck in Austria and on to Zurich and Geneva where he arrived in October,1691. Although only 38 years old, he succumbed to his illness in Geneva where he died in January,1692. His two sons, Thomas and John, together with three valets, travelled to Geneva for the funeral and to settle their father's outstanding bills.

Vice-Chamberlain Thomas Coke, 1675-1727.

Thomas Coke was baptised in Melbourne church on the 19th February, 1675. He was very close to his brother, John, and his three sisters, Elizabeth, Mary and Alice, with whom he maintained a frequent correspondence. At the age of 13, in 1688, he was sent to Rotterdam to be educated by M.Chauvin, a French Protestant minister, where he was taught with other young boys. His school report would be recognised today: "..As he is young, he needs to become a little stimulated...The French language appears difficult to him...." He then went to New College, Oxford.

On reaching his majority in 1696, he returned to Holland and stayed at The Loo with a friend in the household of William of Orange. He became a young man about town, and was fond of the playhouse, poetry, drinking, ladies and the good things of life. He became friendly with Robert Shirley, the son of Earl Ferrers of Staunton Harold, with whom he exchanged ballads and verses. In August, he returned again to Holland, visiting The Loo and Cleves; one of his friends wrote that he was missed "at the Bath and Tunbridge where the ladies shake the elbow..."

In the summer of 1697, Thomas's sisters, Alice Coke and Mary Fanshawe, wrote to say that they were distressed to hear that he had gone to the King's Camp in Holland. It was here that Coke met Lady Mary Stanhope who was accompanying her brother, Philip, one of Coke's drinking partners. Lady Mary was the daugher of the second Earl of Chesterfield whose family home was at Bretby, about 6 miles from Melbourne. After he returned to England, Lord Widdrington wrote from Brussels: "Last night was the first time your charming mistress made her appearance since your departure. Stanhope and I did both make her a compliment from you, which she received with a graceful smile, asking whether you did not come again..." The courtship continued and Thomas and Mary were married at Repton in June, 1698. The indomitable Celia Fiennes was riding past at this time and paid a visit to Bretby where she found "the drawinge roome had company in it - the Earle having just marry'd his eldest Daughter Lady Mary to one Mr Cooke, a Gentleman of a good Estate hard by, so there was company to wishe her joy..."

He had prepared a house in London for his bride, at No.3, St.James's Place. As there were only six rooms, he had an extension built on the back. This caused friction with his neighbour, Charles Godolphin, who objected to the encroachment and threatened to build a high wall as a "monument of malice". At one stage, Mr.Godolphin stood by with a pistol, watching the workmen and threatening to shoot anybody who put a hand over his fence. In August, 1698, Coke was elected member of Parliament for the County of Derby, and immediately received pleas to support the Derwent Navigation and Trent Navigation bills which were proposed for that Session.

Having organised his London home, Thomas then turned his attention to his country house at Melbourne. He had been impressed by the Dutch style of gardens when he spent some of his youth at The Loo. His father-in-law had laid out a series of gardens at Bretby in the style of Versailles, which included a 50 feet water fountain, and these had made a great impression on Thomas. He determined to do the same at Melbourne and in 1698, he ordered a number of lead statues from John Nost, the sculptor, of Piccadilly, and acacias, Dutch elms and fruit trees from Henry Wise's nurseries at Brompton Park. He made a drawing for his garden layout which he discussed with George London, who, with Henry Wise, later became the royal gardeners to Queen Anne. Coke soon realised that any changes could be lost to his family, as he only held the lease on Melbourne Hall, which was the freehold of the Bishop of Carlisle. The workmen at Melbourne were discharged while he negotiated to purchase the freehold from the Bishop. Eventually, in 1704, a Bill was passed through Parliament which gave Coke the freehold of Melbourne, but the chief rent payable to the Bishop of Carlisle was increased.

After his marriage Thomas continued to play his role of man-about-town, with his interests in the theatre, music and drinking. He exchanged poems with his friends, Henry St.John, William Stratford and Matthew Prior, whom he would meet in the London Chocolate houses. A horrifying playbill for 27 April,1702, advertises a dogfight at the Bear Garden in Hockley-in-the-Hole, where an added attraction was "..a great Mad Bull to be turned loose in the Game-place, with Fire-works all over him, and two or three Cats ty'd to his Tail, and Dogs after them..." Coke was concerned with the delights of social life in London and his bills for the wig-maker and suppliers of snuff, tea and chocolate show how important these items were to him. Alexander Pope's lines:

"Sir Plume of amber snuff-box justly vain...."

are thought to refer to the young Thomas Coke.

Thomas Coke, portrait by Michael Dahl.

In February, 1701, a daughter, Mary, was born to Lady Mary Coke. Thomas was in Derbyshire fighting an election for Parliament, in which he was defeated. His friends were upset and said that he had been "baseley used by his own countrey". He considered standing for Leicestershire and was offered a seat in Lancashire. He spent the summer of 1701 in Melbourne with his wife and daughter and was eventually elected in the December election where he topped the poll with 1,659 votes. In March, 1702, the old King, William III, died and Anne became Queen in her own right. Another election was called and in August, Thomas was elected unopposed for Derbyshire. A second daughter, Elizabeth, was born in March,1703. This disappointed his brother-in-law, Lord Stanhope, who wrote: "I believe I might have had a nephew, had it not been prevented by the pernicious influence of too many cucumbers." After the birth of her second child, Lady Mary went to Bath for her health. She was suffering from "cholic" and was prescribed laudanum and quarts of water. Unfortunately she died on 11 January,1704, leaving Thomas a widower, with two young daughters to bring up.

Thomas's younger brother, John, had been touring France, learning the language, in 1701. With the prospect of the War of the Spanish Succession looming, John left Paris for Brussels, observing that "The French are all in motion". In Amsterdam, he wrote: "I never saw such a country for spending money and having nothing for it", and in The Hague: "It is a country which is good for nothing but to pass through". The Dutch were drowning their land at Nijmegen and the British army under their General, the Duke of Marlborough, embarked for The Netherlands. Thomas Coke was friendly with Marlborough, and had many friends in the army, who kept him up-to-date with the fortunes of the war. Coke had asked Marlborough to find him a position in the Court, and on April 3, 1704, before he left England, Marlborough wrote that he had suggested some positions to the Queen. Marlborough was victorious at Blenheim on August 2nd, 1704, and the French Marshal Tallard was captured and brought to England. Coke accepted a position in the Government as one of the Tellers of the Exchequer, but it was not until the end of 1706 that Marlborough obtained for him the prestigious situation of the Vice-Chamberlain to Her Majesty's Household.

In the summer of 1702, Sir John and Lady Catherine Harpur had stayed at Melbourne Hall, while their house at Calke was being rebuilt. Their servants stayed on until 1703 and the house then remained empty apart from occasional visits by Thomas who was now ready to recommence his garden work. Thomas was also fond of visiting his old friend, Walter Burdett, in his quiet retreat at Knowl Hills in Ticknall.

After their mother's death, his two daughters were looked after by his unmarried sisters, Elizabeth and Alice. Daughter Mary stayed with Lady Catherine Clarke at Wing where she was taken ill, due to eating paper, acorns and green apples with Miss Katie Bertie, "a little ringleader to mischief". In the spring of 1705, Elizabeth took his daughters to Melbourne Hall where they lived for several years and she was able to keep a watch on the development of the gardens. Michael Dahl was commissioned to paint a portrait of the two girls, but he found it quite difficult: "...she [Mary] has sat for the first time for her picture with a great deal of good humour, but so very much motion, that put Mr Dahl upon great difficulty.." and again "...no contrivance that we could think of could prevail with her to be half a moment at a time in a posture..." The finished portrait can be seen on the staircase at Melbourne Hall.

Having obtained the freehold of Melbourne Hall, Thomas set to work to implement his new garden plans. A gang of bricklayers, masons, carpenters and gardeners descended on the Hall. Elizabeth Coke, now in

"Andromeda"

"Perseus"

"The Quarrelling Boys"

"The Four Seasons"

John Nost's Lead Statues in Melbourne Hall Gardens

residence at Melbourne, commented on "the dust and noisy work of your gardens". John Nost's lead statues were arranged according to Thomas's plan and a Derbyshire ironsmith, Robert Bakewell, was commissioned to construct an Iron Arbour ("The Birdcage") to close the view along the main avenue of the gardens.

London & Wise supplied the shrubs, evergreens and fruit trees from their Brompton Park nurseries. Queen Anne herself, commissioned a vase from John Nost, which depicted the Four Seasons and cost £100. William Cooke of Walcot was employed as the gardener to oversee the layout of the parterres and lawns. Sir John Coke's dovecot was converted into a Library for Thomas's books (now the Muniment Room). A washhouse and bakehouse was built outside the garden wall (now the Tea Rooms). The water supply to the fountains was designed by George Sorocold, who had built the waterworks to the Derby Silk Mill and London Bridge. They were fed directly from Melbourne Pool by raising the level of the Pool. By 1708, most of the works had been completed.

Robert Bakewell had built his iron forge in the basement of the Stone House, near Melbourne Church. After he had finished the Iron Arbour, he continued to work there on commissions for Staunton Harold church, Foremark and Cholmondeley Castle. By 1711, Elizabeth was preparing to return to London with Thomas's daughters. She had made the Hall safe, but Mr.Bakewell was still in the Stone House. "...He is so miserably poor that I believe he cannot remove till he has some money. He has got a shop fitting up at Derby. So far as 5£ I have promised to let him have..."

Thomas paid occasional visits to Melbourne while the garden work was going on. He had to be there for the elections of 1705 and 1708 when he was returned as member for Derbyshire. In 1705, his bachelor friend, Henry St.John, now Secretary at War, wrote: "Dear Rake, I am glad to hear your election is over, your feavour gone, and your worship is again upon the hunt: for what the devil can carry you to the Bath at this time but a whore?..." Another item of gossip informed Coke that Lord Delaware's mother-in-law had married her postman. The following year, William Stratford, now a Chaplain at Christ Church, Oxford, wrote: "..You may now have leisure to finish your fine gardens and when they are done, you may sit in security under your own vines and fig trees..."

Coke sent champagne and books to Marshal Tallard, who had been taken prisoner at the Battle of Blenheim and was now held at Nottingham. In 1705, Elizabeth was at Bretby, when Marshal Tallard arrived for dinner with the Earl of Chesterfield. The Queen had no objection to Coke seeing Tallard, and Tallard surprised Coke by visiting him at Melbourne.

However, Thomas's visits to Melbourne ceased abruptly, when, in 1706, he was appointed a Privy Councillor and Vice-Chamberlain to the Queen's Household. His duties kept him in St.James's, Kensington Palace and Hampton Court, where he was required to organise the affairs of the Household. He was responsible for the purchase and arrangement of the pictures and books at the Royal palaces. Coke had a scheme for boarding up the tennis court at Hampton Court in the winter, to make a room for card playing, but this was rejected on the grounds of cost.

It was at Court that Thomas met Mary Hale, the daughter of William Hale of Kings Walden, Herts., who was a Maid of Honour to the Queen. This post had been obtained for her by Sarah, Duchess of Marlborough. They were married in October, 1709. Thomas's daughters by his first marriage were excited at the thought of meeting their new mother, and Elizabeth was ready to move from Melbourne back to London to deliver up her charges. In February, 1714, a daughter, Anne, was born but she died at the age of 6 months and was buried in St. James's Vaults, London. A post mortem revealed that she was choked by the remains of an "apostem" in the lung. A son, George Lewis, was born in March, 1715, and a daughter, Charlotte, in January, 1720. All three children were born in Melbourne.

The 1710 election was coloured by the preachings of Dr.Sacheverell, who stated that the Church was in danger due to the presence of Dissenters encouraged by the Queen. The gentlemen of Derbyshire met secretly at Swarkestone to select their candidates and asked Thomas Coke to make his position clear. Coke continued his resolution of standing but did not visit Derbyshire to meet the electors, due to his service to the Queen. His absence was misrepresented and although sister Elizabeth tried to drum up support for him, she claimed that by not coming up, his interest declined daily. Even his friend, John Hardinge of Kings Newton, was neutral. Eventually, the electors chose Mr.Curzon and Mr.Clarke to represent them. Thomas was accepted as the candidate for Grampound, a pocket borough in Cornwall. The vicar there was pleased to have a member who could be entrusted to deliver those secret messages to the Queen to prevent the Whigs getting the ascendant and bringing the Church into danger.

Peace with France was proclaimed in 1713, and in August,1714, Queen Anne died and George of Hanover became King. At the interment of the Queen, Coke was appointed to assist the two Duchesses who were to bear the Chief Mourner's Train. King George I confirmed Thomas Coke in his position of Vice-Chamberlain to the Household.

Thomas's life now seems to have become less hectic and he was able to devote some time to his interest in gardens. He designed the garden layout for the Earl of Berkeley at Cranford, Middlesex, as well as a summer house at Kingsweston for his son-in-law, Viscount Southwell, a chapel at Drayton for Lady Betty Germain and an obelisk at Blenheim for the Duke of Marlborough. He also did some more work in his Melbourne gardens and some alterations to Melbourne Hall itself. The hall was in a poor condition and, in 1708, the floors had been propped up in the maid's chamber, the servants' hall and the nursery. Elizabeth Coke thought that, with all its props, "...the house with all its faults would last longer yet than perhaps any now alive would want it..."

In 1720, new trees were obtained for the gardens, and the New Intake was planted with a hundred chestnuts. A team of gardeners was employed to look after the gardens. 6 gardeners and 4 labourers were paid 8d. a day each, and 4 female weeders were employed at 4d. a day each. William Gilks of Burton-on-Trent was employed to make good the house roof and to build new stairs and chimneys. New sash windows with shutters were fitted. In 1722, the estate was mapped by Thomas Kirkland. In 1723, Thomas wrote that he intended a seat by the wall by Mill Fleam "if ever I live to see Melborne". He subscribed £50 for the rebuilding of All Saints Church, Derby in 1723. In 1725, he employed Francis Smith of Warwick to build a gatehouse near the entrance by the church. The agent observed that during the construction: "next to the Chancel, we fell into an old burying place where we found a great many human bones".

In 1720, Thomas Coke was given the sinecure post of Surveyor of His Majesty's Customs. He was responsible for the taxes collected on wine, tobacco, coffee, coals, cinders and whale fins. He was involved in the creation of the new order of Knights of the Bath in 1725. That same year, the stock in the South Sea Company collapsed (the "South Sea Bubble") and Thomas Coke's syndicate sold £534 of stock "for any consideration and sum of money whatsoever".

Thomas Coke died suddenly, at the early age of 52, on 16 May, 1727, leaving behind three daughters and a young son. His body was carried to Melbourne for burial. His effects which were sold by auction at Covent Garden in 1728, included: "several thousand ounces of fashionable plate, jewels, mathematical instruments and other valuable curiosities".

George Lewis Coke, 1715-1750.

George Lewis Coke was born in 1715, the only son of Thomas Coke, and therefore his natural heir. He had a sister, Charlotte, five years younger than himself and two half sisters, Mary who married Viscount Southwell, and Elizabeth, who married Bache Thornhill. He was only 12 years old when his father died and his uncle, John Coke of Gray's Inn, together with Thomas's brother-in-law, John Hardinge of Kings Newton were appointed his guardians. Matthew Lamb, a lawyer, of Lincolns Inn, looked after the legal implications.

George was brought up in London, and at the age of 7, he was taught to write and to dance. When he was 10, uncle John wrote that he had an illness in his eyes from which he recovered. His sister, Charlotte, known as "Pud", was well. When he was 15, John noted that his nephew was longing to see Melbourne, which he did that year. At the age of 17, he was admitted to the post of Surveyor-General of His Majesty's Customs, which had been held by his father and then administered by his guardians. In 1732, he went to Christ Church College, Oxford, having bought two "pretty nags", and in the following year, he visited Melbourne again.

In July, 1734, he set off on The Grand Tour of Europe, to broaden his education. Uncle John kept Joseph Greaves, the Melbourne agent informed of his progress. His route kept him out of the way of the armies and he rode by Paris and Bordeaux to Montpellier where he spent the winter. The following year he went on to Rome and Naples, where John Coke wrote that: "...he has not ailed anything since he left England..." In June, 1735, he was in Venice and "...galloping away to Vienna with an Intention to go through Germany to Holland & from thence thro Flanders to Paris. He will have many a bad day's Journey & worse Inns...but his Curiosity will cost him money..." In 1736, John Coke confessed that he had not heard from his nephew for three weeks "...but expect it very soon, unlesse he has the secret of Liveing without money..." George Lewis returned to England after his twenty month tour of the Continent.

He never married and moved to Melbourne to live the life of a country gentleman and to continue his father's plans for Melbourne Hall and Gardens. He planted part of Dovemore, opposite Melbourne Pool, with trees and built a summer house there. Thomas Coke had never completed the east facade of Melbourne Hall, and George employed William Smith of Warwick to do the design work. In 1743, 10 guineas was "paid Mr Smith of Warwick for Journeys & makeing Draught & Estimate of Melbourne House".The east front was restricted to only 7 bays, whereas Thomas had intended a longer front of 11 bays. William Jackson agreed to pull down some old building and erect the new east front for a sum of £1,500. This was completed in 1744. Repair work continued and in 1748, Greaves was searching for bricklayers as far afield as Ashby-de-la-Zouch and Diseworth.

On 22 November, 1745, George Lewis Coke was appointed Deputy-Lieutenant of Derbyshire and would thus have been involved in Bonnie Prince Charlie's march to Derby, but no information relating to this incident has survived. On 15 January,1751, Matthew Lamb wrote from London to William Fox, the Melbourne agent: "My brother Coke your master died yesterday morning. His illness lasted some time and he left no will. All his estates are come to me in the right of my wife [Charlotte] who is his sister and heir...The Funerall is to be at Melbourne in the Burying Place of the family in the Church which I would have to be as near as convenience will admit to the Place his father was Buryed in..." Lamb gave full instructions for the Funeral and the cold dinner for the refreshment after the ceremony. George Lewis Coke was buried in Melbourne church on 24 January, 1751.

George Lewis Coke.
on The Grand Tour
Portrait by Pompeo Botoni

Sir Matthew Lamb, Bt., 1704-1768.

Peniston Lamb of Southwell, Nottinghamshire, built up a flourishing lawyer's business and when he died in 1734, his goods and chambers in Lincoln's Inn, London, were left to his nephew, Matthew, who was also a lawyer. His wealth, thought to be about £100,000, went mainly to Matthew as residual legatee. Matthew's brother, Robert, made his life in the church, and later became the Bishop of Peterborough.

Matthew was a thrusting, ambitious member of the "nouveau-riche" and was poles apart from the gentle, leisurely lifestyle of Thomas Coke. He acted as lawyer for Sir Robert Sutton in his purchase of estates in Nottinghamshire and Lincolnshire, and also as legal advisor to James, the sixth Earl of Salisbury, who lived at Hatfield House, Hertfordshire. In April, 1740, Matthew married Charlotte, the sister of George Lewis

Coke, and looked after the legal business of the Melbourne estates for Coke. A daughter, Charlotte, was born in November, 1743, and a son, Peniston, in January, 1748. Another daughter, Ann, died young.

Perhaps it was through his friendship with Lord Salisbury at Hatfield, that Matthew decided to purchase the nearby estate of Brocket, from the Reade family in 1746. Matthew had the old manor house demolished and built the present Brocket Hall, with its park and ornamental lakes, from designs by James Payne. Brocket Hall was conveniently close to London and became the favoured seat of most of the succeeding Lambs, whilst the residence at Melbourne Hall was now only used on rare occasions.

Brocket Hall, near Hatfield, Hertfordshire

In 1752, Sir Robert Sutton's estates, for which Matthew Lamb had negotiated twenty years earlier, came on the market. After a careful study of their profitability, Matthew purchased the estates of Greasley, Selston and Bulwell in Nottinghamshire and Boothby Graffoe in Lincolnshire for the sum of £46,986. This property was added to the Melbourne Rental. The agent, William Fox, not only had to supervise Over Haddon, 35 miles north and Duston, which was 56 miles to the south, but now had to travel to Boothby Graffoe, which was over 50 miles to the east. The Greasley and Selston estates later became very important with the development of their coal mines.

Matthew was created a Baronet in 1755 and wrote to Fox that he was "sent for suddenly to come here to kisse the Kings hand, he having done me the honour to create me a Baronet..." The following year, another honour came his way: "The King having been pleased to appoint me to be Custos Rotulorum [Keeper of the Rolls] of the Liberty of Peterborough in the Room of the late Earl Fitzwilliam..." When King George II died, he noted in a letter of 2 November,1760, that: "The sudden death of the King has put things in a hurry..."

It was a period of change. The Enclosure of the medieval open fields could be obtained by Act of Parliament and the tarmacadamed Turnpike Roads were rapidly penetrating the countryside. He approved the Enclosure of Melton Mowbray in 1760, and in 1764, when the Enclosure of Barrow-upon-Trent was proposed, he wrote to Fox: "I shan't object if I make a profit - not a mere exchange of a pennyworth for my penny..." However he couldn't agree terms and the Enclosure of Barrow was delayed until 1787. He was keen to pursue the Enclosure of Bakewell, as he was the second largest land owner in the parish, but the Duke of Rutland objected and Matthew commented laconically: "...Don't know why. I was willing to agree to it on the terms proposed..."

There was a problem with the Title to the Fishery at Barrow, when Mrs. Sale and the Reverend Mr. Astilly were found fishing with nets in the Trent at Barrow. Mrs. Sale claimed to have fishing rights formerly held by the Priory of Caulke. However, Matthew brought the full weight of the law into action and threatened Mrs. Sale with a court case; he was able to prove his Title easily. Mrs. Sale then admitted trespass and Matthew agreed to drop his proceedings. Her attempt to sell his fishery was "too gross an insult to be putt upp with easily..."

In 1759, Matthew wrote: "I am in generall a friend to Turnpikes knowing that good roads can't be had without them..." He was directly involved when the London to Derby road was turnpiked. Crossing of the Trent was by the means of Wilne Ferry, a part of the Manor of Castle Donington and the property of Lamb, but by 1758, the traffic increase generated by the turnpike road was too much for the ferry. A bridge was proposed by the Duke of Devonshire and a Trust set up to construct the bridge, which was to be known as Cavendish Bridge. Matthew approved the bridge, which was designed by James Paine, and was making a handsome profit out of the sale of his ferry rights. On 5 February, 1761, Matthew wrote to Fox: "I understand Wilden Ferry bridge is quite finished, and is reckoned to be very well done. My boats are therefore of no use to the Ferry. Take them into your custody and sell them..."

Matthew Lamb continued to purchase property, notably in Ab Kettleby and Sysonby in Leicestershire in 1762, as well as small farms at Chellaston, Willington and Kings Newton. In 1758, Mrs. Alice Hardinge died and her estate at Kings Newton and Linton passed to Matthew. Alice was a link with the past; she was Thomas Coke's sister and

Charlotte Lamb's aunt and had married John Hardinge of Kings Newton in 1711. When John Hardinge died, she held the estates in Jointure and when she died, it reverted to Matthew as the inheritor of the Coke estates.

Matthew lived mainly in Sackville Street, London and Brocket Hall, Hatfield, and rarely visited Melbourne. On one occasion, he wrote: "I am now settled at this place [Brocket] with my family for the summer and don't find any disposition in myself to leave it to go to Melbourn where I can't yet bring myself to go without being uneasy..." His daughter, Charlotte, married Henry Belasyse, the son of the Earl of Fauconberg, and this event was connected with one of Matthew's rare visits to Melbourne. On 17 July, 1768, he wrote: "I intend to be at Melbourn the 1st week in August for about a week, Lord and Lady Belasyse, who are now here, and Mr Lamb will come with me...Tell Sands I expect the gardens to be in order...Get some small beer as there will be a good many servants..." Further instructions arrived with Matthew's keen eye for detail: "The Red Room next the Pool for Lord and Lady Belasyse, the room next the garden for Mr Lamb, my own room as usual, the rooms over the kitchen for the cook and servants, Lady Belasyse's maid may lie in the Blue Room next the garden..." Final details arrived: "I intend to be at Melbourn next Wednesday...The beds must be well aired. The weather is vastly hot..."

ADVERTISEMENT.

September 6, 1754.

WHEREAS, on *Monday* Night, the 12th of *August* laſt, the large POND at MELBOURNE, in the County of *DERBY*, belonging to MATTHEW LAMB, Eſq; was robb'd of a great Quantity of PIKE and BREAM: And whereas a WARRANT hath iſſued for apprehending *Chriſtopher Richardſon*, of the Borough of *DERBY*, *Cooper*, for the ſame, who hath ſince abſconded; and ſeveral other Perſons being ſuſpected to be concerned in the ſaid Robbery: *This is therefore to give Notice*, That whoever ſhall give Information of the ſaid *Richardſon*, or any other Perſon, guilty of the ſaid Robbery, ſo that he or they may be apprehended, ſhall receive the Sum of TEN GUINEAS, upon his or their Conviction; to be paid by Mr. WILLIAM FOX, at MELBOURNE aforeſaid, or Mr. JOSEPH HAYNE, Attorney at Law in *DERBY*.

N. B. The ſaid *Chriſt. Richardſon* is a broadiſh ſet Man, about five Feet ten Inches high, upwards of fifty Years of Age, and ſtoops in the Shoulders; has a Scar upon one Cheek, and a largiſh red Noſe, with a deep hoarſe Voice, and wore a White Drill Frock.

Memo: There was 300 of these advertisements printed and Dispersed and was also published in the Derby News Paper at the same time.

This visit happened shortly after the death of Matthew's wife, Charlotte, the last of the Cokes, in June., 1768. Matthew did not long survive his wife as a letter from Peniston Lamb, dated 7 November, 1768, asked Fox to go into mourning for Sir Matthew Lamb, who had died the previous day. He was buried in Hatfield church, alongside the tombs of the Brockets, whose lands he had purchased twenty years earlier. He was said to have been worth £500,000 in property and £500.000 in cash, when he died.

Peniston Lamb, 1748-1828.
First Viscount Melbourne.

Peniston Lamb was born on 9th January, 1748, the only son of Matthew and Charlotte. He was only 20 years old when his father died, and the inheritance of Matthew's vast wealth as well as his title, opened up all the joys of London to this pleasure-seeking young man. He seemed determined to spend his wealth as quickly as possible upon drinking, gambling, and hunting, and, in this, he was capably aided by his mistress, Mrs. Sophia Baddeley.

In London society, he encountered a 17-year old provincial girl, who was becoming renowned for her beauty and wit. This was Elizabeth Milbanke, the daughter of Sir Ralph Milbanke of Halnaby Hall in Croft-on-Tees in north Yorkshire. Above all, Elizabeth was ambitious, and in Peniston, she saw a rather weak, young man, with ample money to fulfil her ambitions of recognition in the world of pleasure and fashion. With the connivance of Peniston's sister, Charlotte, they were married in April, 1769. In April, 1770, he was created an Irish peer, and took for his title: "Lord Melbourne, Baron of Kilmore in the County of Cavan". Writing to his Melbourne agent on 10 April, 1770, he observed: "His Majesty having been pleased to create me a Peer of Ireland, I thought it proper to take my title from Melbourne, it's very agreeable to me as I look upon it as a step to an English Peerage in some future time..."

Shortly afterwards, a son, named Peniston after his father, was born. Peniston's house in Sackville Street was adequate for his debauched bachelor days, but it was not grand enough for Elizabeth and in 1771, they moved to Lord Holland's house in Piccadilly, which they renamed Melbourne House. It is now known as "Albany". Peniston and Elizabeth now seemed to go their separate ways; she had produced his son and heir and he could now retire to his passions for horses, gambling and eating.
He commissioned a painting from Joseph Wright of Derby in October, 1770: "Mr. Wright of Derby...had a draft...for one hundred guineas. So I

would have you pay it him immediately and it is worth your while when you go to Derby to see the Picture he is painting for me. It is thought to be the best ever painted in this country..." The painting is "A Blacksmith's Shop" and is now in the Paul Mellon collection at Yale.

Meanwhile, Elizabeth frequented the Carlton House set, led by George, Prince of Wales. In this colourful, romantic and extravagant society, manners were always superior to morals and "wife swapping" was commonplace. Lord Melbourne did not seem to want any more children, so Lady Melbourne had to look elsewhere and at the age of 27, she gave birth to another son, William, in 1779, who was probably fathered by Lord Egremont. In 1782, Frederic was born, and the choice of name can be seen as a compliment to the King's son, Frederic, Duke of York. There seems less doubt about the parentage of the next son, George, who was born in 1784, as the result of a brief liaison with George, Prince of Wales. Peniston's lawyer, Thomas Hill, wrote to William Fox at Melbourne: "Lady Melbourne got a fine boy on Sunday sennight the Eleventh instant ...This ought to make my Lord think of Frugality, but as a Notable Noble Lord observed to me: a Great House makes a bad Figure without Suitable Living..."

Lord Melbourne watched his growing family with interest. A daughter, Emily, was born in 1787, and she was thought to be either an Act of God, or, more likely, Lord Egremont again. The family was completed when another daughter, Harriett, was born in 1789.

Lord Melbourne's Children
Peniston, Frederic & William.
Portrait by Joshua Reynolds

The original is at Firle Park, Lewes, Sussex.

Peniston took little interest in estate matters apart from his twice yearly visit to Melbourne to collect the rents. Kings Newton Hall was leased to Edward Abney and Mr. Abney complained that the gamekeeper, Charles Bowman had been insolent to him and his company on Derby Hills. Lord Melbourne pointed out that the liberty to shoot was given only to Abney and not to his visitors and friends. Bowman continued to stop Abney who complained again to Peniston; Peniston asked Bowman not to be so saucy, but wrote that he believed Mr. Abney was quite mad. Abney later requested the removal of a large sawpit near his house, which had greatly endangered Mrs. Abney's life, and when Abney started cutting down trees, Peniston wrote: "I find fault with Mr. Abney having cut down the Elm Tree; you did right to inform me of it. He is a very odd man tho' at the same time a very good tenant so I have not been harsh with him..."

As one of the major landowners in Melbourne, Peniston was involved in the Enclosure of 1787, along with the Earl of Huntingdon and others. In 1789, he complained bitterly: "The Melbourne Rent has so far advanced only £383.12.10. from the Inclosure. Is this the whole advantage to be expected from such an expensive business..." The Melbourne agent, William Fox, was succeeded by his son, Henry, in 1788.

Lord Melbourne was promoted from an Irish Baron to an Irish Viscount in 1781 and was made a Lord of the Bedchamber to the Prince of Wales (later George IV) in 1784. The Prince presented him with Joshua Reynold's portrait of the Prince of Wales standing by his charger: this portrait still hangs above the fireplace in the Dining Room at Brocket Hall. In 1792, Melbourne House in Piccadilly was exchanged for the Duke of York's house in Whitehall, which was located between the Horse Guards and the Treasury Office. Lady Melbourne immediately renamed it Melbourne House. The Old Lottery Office was demolished and a new coach house erected. It is now the Scottish Office. At the new Melbourne House, Lady Melbourne continued to be the hostess for the grand Whig balls and parties, which had been a feature of the old Melbourne House in Piccadilly.

With both Lord and Lady Melbourne's profligate spending, not even Matthew Lamb's fortune would last forever, and, after 1800, Peniston started selling his estates to maintain his life style. The main bulk of the estates could not be sold, as by his Marriage Settlement, they were entailed to each of their children in turn. Nevertheless some estates had missed the entail, and he was able to sell Bolsterstone and Langsett in Yorkshire and Wilsford in Lincolnshire. The Enclosure of Chellaston in 1802, provided the opportunity for selling his significant holdings there.

In 1803, Lord Melbourne's heir, young Peniston, was 33 years old and still unmarried, although he had been having an affair with Mrs. Musters at Colwick, near Nottingham. Disaster was soon to strike Melbourne House. In that same year, Harriett died of consumption at the age of 14. Two years later, young Peniston himself, the apple of his father's eye, was also struck down with consumption. In accord with the morals of the time, Lady Melbourne summoned Mrs. Musters to Peniston's death bed. The death of Peniston junior, left the second son, William, heir to the title and the Melbourne properties.

Within a few months, the gloom had lifted when Lady Melbourne was able to announce the marriage of her eldest son and her only daughter. On 27 May, 1805, she wrote to Henry Fox in Melbourne: "I find Hassard [the agent at Brocket Hall] did not believe the paragraph he saw in the papers about William's marriage, it is fact & I believe they will be married on Monday next, the lady is Lady Caroline Ponsonby daughter to Lord Bessborough. Emily is also going to be married to Lord Cowper and we are extremely happy at both marriages..." This happiness was not to last when the true nature of Lady Caroline became evident.

Lord and Lady Melbourne were enthusiastic about Whig politics and both supported the war against France. In 1803, Lord Melbourne made a subscription to the Greasley Volunteers and provided £25 for clothing the 120 Volunteers from Melbourne. In 1804, Mr. Abney of Kings Newton wrote to say that the Volunteers were appearing at church in their new uniforms and wished to drink the health of the family at the Hall. Peniston told Fox: "Fix a date; you might do it at about 2s. a head. Give them as much of my ale as they can drink..."

On 6 November, 1805, Lady Melbourne sent to Fox a copy of the London Gazette Extraordinary, with an account of the Battle of Trafalgar: "I send you a Gazette which will go free & I think you will like to read an account of this glorious victory which has caused great rejoicings here, although a gloom is thrown over the whole by the loss of Lord Nelson, which must be sincerely and deservedly regretted by the whole nation..." After the Battle of Talavera, she described the scene in London in a letter of 14 August, 1809: "The Guns in the Park are now firing on account of a Victory obtained by Sir Arthur Wellesley [later Duke of Wellington] over the French in Spain commanded by Joseph Buonaparte in person. The Battle lasted two days and the loss is great on both sides - ours is 5376 killed & wounded 2 missing. The French are computed to have lost 11,000 men..."

It is probable that Lady Melbourne was responsible for organising the marriages of William and Emily. She was less successful in obtaining a bride for Frederic, but she used her influence with the Prince of Wales to obtain him the position of a cornet in the Royal Horse Guards. However, Frederic eventually joined the Diplomatic Service. She was more successful with her other son, George, introducing him to Caroline St. Jules, who was the result of an affair between the Duke of Devonshire and Lady Elizabeth Foster. They were married on 17 May, 1809.

Lord Melbourne scarcely used Melbourne Hall and decided to raise cash by letting it. Sir William Rumbold took a lease of the Hall in 1811, but did not occupy it fully and relinquished his lease in 1815. His son-in-law, Sir Sydney Smith, who had defeated Bonaparte at the Siege of Acre, lived there for some time. Melbourne Hall was not then fully occupied again until George Lamb retired to live there in 1824. George made several changes to the house and gardens until his death in 1834.

In 1815, Lord Melbourne received the ultimate accolade of an English Viscountcy, a title which his wife had long desired. Finding the money for the fees perplexed Lord Melbourne as he wrote to Fox on 15 August, 1815: "The call for as much as £600 fees for my patent of Peerage has distressed me at present as the fees must be settled before the Patent is given out. Cookney [the family lawyer] thinks getting the money a concern of the family. It would not be improper to cut some wood for it & I want to know if you know how you could in different places at a proper time cut for that sum without diminishing the Annual fall for if you could do that & know at what time the money or such sale would be forthcoming, I could then get money advanced..."

In 1818, Lady Melbourne was taken ill and the family rallied round. On 26 March, George Lamb wrote to Fox: "As they put in the newspaper that Lord Melbourne is seriously indisposed at his house in Whitehall, he desires me just to write this, to tell you that he is neither confined nor indisposed but Lady Melbourne continues ill..." On 6 April, a letter arrived from William Lamb: "I have to inform you of the melancholy event of Lady Melbourne's decease, which took place this morning - her end was tranquil and free from pain, but the suffering of her illness had been great - you will communicate this sad intelligence to Mr. Middleton [the vicar] & all at Melbourne..." It was William, who, in later life, summed up his mother's character as "A remarkable woman, a devoted mother, an excellent wife - but not chaste, not chaste."

After the death of his wife, Peniston seems to have retired into a reclusive, perhaps alcoholic state, leaving his son, William, and the family lawyer, Charles Cookney, to administer the estates. He lived on another ten years, and it was on the 23rd July, 1828, that William Lamb wrote to Henry Fox to tell him that Lord Melbourne had died and gave instructions for the mourning. The vast numbers of bills that Peniston had incurred during the last ten years were all unpaid and William had the problem of finding the money to pay them.

William Lamb, 1779-1848.
Second Viscount Melbourne.

William Lamb was born on 15 March, 1779, the second son of Peniston and Elizabeth. His early life was spent in the two Melbourne Houses in Piccadilly and Whitehall, with occasional visits to their country house, Brocket Hall, in Hertfordshire. He was educated at Eton and Trinity College, Cambridge. Wars in France rendered the Grand Tour impossible so he rounded off his education in Glasgow. Because he was the second son and was not expected to inherit the estates and title, it was decided that he should take up a legal career, and he was admitted to the Bar in 1804. However, his prospects changed when his elder brother, Peniston, died in 1805 and William became Lord Melbourne's heir.

William then changed his profession from the Law to Politics and a safe Parliamentary seat was found for him at Leominster., He was now sufficiently wealthy to think about marriage. As good Whigs, the Lamb family were great friends of the Duke & Duchess of Devonshire, who occupied Devonshire House in Piccadilly, not far from Melbourne House. Lady Bessborough was sister to the Duchess of Devonshire and lived in Devonshire House with her family, with other offspring of the Duke. The Countess of Bessborough's daughter, Lady Caroline Ponsonby, was born in 1785 and seems to have met William Lamb on a visit to Brocket Hall

Lady Melbourne

The Honourable William Lamb

Lady Caroline Lamb

in 1801. William was struck by her large eyes and elfin face and by her vivacious charm. Her strange personality was expressed by her nick-names, "Ariel", "Sprite" and "Savage". Caroline admired William's kind and gentle character and his love of liberty and independence.

They were married at Devonshire House on 3 June, 1805 in the presence of all the Whig hierarchy. The honeymoon at Brocket was not a success as Caroline was taken ill, a hint of the nervous depression which dominated her life. A premature child was still-born in January, 1806 and a son, Augustus, in September, 1807. The Prince Regent acted as godfather, but Augustus was a sickly child; he was mentally retarded and subject to frequent fits. He must have been a great trial to his parents and was said to have a mental age of seven when he died in 1836. Another attempt at a child resulted in a still-born baby in February, 1809. Caroline's love for babies can be seen in her sketches which are on display in Melbourne Hall.

Caroline paid her first visit to Melbourne in 1806, and Lady Melbourne had, by now, become acquainted with the eccentricities of her daughter-in-law, She wrote to Henry Fox: "As she was never at Melbourne before, I beg you will speak to her when keeping out all the idle people with which the House will be fill'd if she is not cautioned against it..." Lord Melbourne wrote: "Let me know when some measures are taken to prevent people peeping under the garden wall at Melbourne..."

Lord Melbourne passed over the running of his estates to William, but William was busy with Parliamentary business. He used his Melbourne agent to obtain information for him, a technique he later found useful when he was Prime Minister. On 7 February, 1812, at the time of the Luddite smashing of stocking-frames in the Midlands, he wrote to Fox: "...let me know if any outrages have been committed at Melbourne...If you could obtain any information of the mode of their organisation, it would be of the greatest service & of course the most inviolate secrecy will be preserved...You will communicate to no one alive what I have written to you upon this subject..." However, William was having trouble with his wife, and he resigned his seat at the 1812 election.

Lord Byron entered London society with the publication of his book "Childe Harold" in 1812. Lady Caroline Lamb had just got over an affair with Sir Godfrey Webster and she was captivated by this new star who took London by storm. She wrote in her diary that she thought Byron was "Mad, bad and dangerous to know". Byron became a constant visitor to Melbourne House and Caroline's wild balls and parties, but Lady Melbourne persuaded Byron to break off the affair. Caroline became desperate and pleaded with Byron not to leave her and made a half-hearted attempt at suicide. Lady Melbourne arranged for Byron to marry her niece, Annabella Milbanke, and they were married at Seaham County Durham, in 1815. Caroline got her revenge by publishing her novel "Glenarvon" which was a thinly disguised story of her affair with Byron. The Lamb family were horrified and arranged a separation between William and Caroline. At the last moment, Caroline pleaded with William not to sign the document and he forgave her. Having come to terms with his wife, William returned to Parliament at the 1816 election as M.P. for Northampton.

The country was in a deep depression and the poor were in a revolutionary mood. Wiliam wrote to Fox: "...poor rates increase in a swift and alarming manner. This presses hard upon the Land owners, forcing their tenants again to depress the manufacturers by diminishing the consumption of their goods & thus to increase the number of the Poor." Fox was able to provide information on the Pentrich Uprising of 1817 and received a petition from the Frame-work Knitters of Melbourne in 1819. However, William Lamb's answer was no comfort: the government could do nothing to relieve the distress and they could only wait for things to get better.

Caroline's mother, Lady Bessborough, died in Florence in 1821 and was brought back to Derby for burial. William and Caroline stayed at the Duke of Devonshire's Derby house for the funeral, and afterwards visited Melbourne. William instructed Fox: "It is of course possible that Lady Caroline may be ill, so as not to be able to come. If we should you will be good enough to take care that there is no ringing of bells nor any thing of that nature". In 1824, Lord Byron died in Greece and when his body was carried to Hucknall, it is recorded that Caroline met the funeral procession when out riding. This seemed to have deranged Caroline completely so that even easy-going William could stand it no longer and signed the Deed of Separation. William allowed her to continue to live at Brocket Hall with their son Augustus, from where she had an affair with Bulwer Lytton from nearby Knebworth. She became a prey to drugs and drink and was taken ill in 1827. She never recovered and William, who was Secretary to Ireland, hurried home from Dublin to see her before she died in January, 1828. She was buried in Hatfield church.

William's younger brother, George, was a keen theatre-goer; he had himself written some unsuccessful plays and had translated the Latin poems of Caius Catullus. He was also a Member of Parliament and helped William in Parliamentary matters. In 1824, he moved to Melbourne Hall with his wife, Caroline, and lived there until he died ten years later. During this period he built up the Library and his inventory of 27th January, 1834, shows that he possessed 2,650 books.

William Lamb had been made Principal Secretary of State for Ireland in Canning's government, where he had some success in dealing with the Nationalists under O'Connell. In Ireland, he became friendly with Lady Brandon who was estranged from her husband. Lord Brandon brought an action against William, but this was dismissed for lack of evidence. When Canning died and that arch-Tory, the Duke of Wellington, was made Prime Minister, William resigned his post. His father died in July, 1828 and William was automatically elevated to the House of Lords as the second Viscount Melbourne. He inherited not only the Melbourne and Brocket Estates, but also his father's vast debts which had to be paid off. He made a start by selling Melbourne House in Whitehall in 1830 and went to live in a bachelor flat in South Street, Mayfair. The manor of Bulwell in Nottinghamshire had been omitted from the Entail of his father's Marriage Settlement, so he was able to sell this in 1833.

King George IV died in 1830 and the new King, William IV, was a Tory and made no secret of his dislike for Lord Melbourne. At the General Election, Wellington was defeated and the King asked Lord Grey to form a Whig government. In this administration, Lord Melbourne became Home Secretary and Lord Palmerston was Foreign Secretary. The country was in a turmoil, there was a strong desire for Parliamentary reform and agricultural labourers were smashing their threshing machines. A Reform Bill to abolish Rotten Boroughs and to extend the franchise, was introduced, but was rejected by the House of Lords. Under pressure from the King, the Lords passed the Bill, which was followed by the first Factories Act and the Poor Law Amendment Act. Nonetheless, unrest and rioting continued. In 1834, a group of Dorset labourers swore a secret oath, which was illegal, and were sentenced by the courts for transportation to Australia. In spite of strong pressure to overrule the court, Lord Melbourne, as Home Secretary, upheld the decision. Now known as the Tolpuddle Martyrs, the labourers were given a general pardon by Melbourne, when he became Prime Minister.

Lord Grey's government fell and the King had no option but to ask Lord Melbourne to be Prime Minister. Henry Fox wrote to him from Melbourne: "I beg to congratulate your Lordship on your having become the head of his majesty's government, an event which has given peculiar satisfaction in this place & neighbourhood..." It seems likely that William was not keen on being Prime Minister; he was free of dogma and had problems in making decisions as he could always see both sides of a question. He was a believer in "laisser faire" policies and objected to major changes. Above all, he enjoyed good food and good company in convivial surroundings. As he was fairly popular with both Whigs and Tories, he made an ideal coalition leader. After six months, William IV dismissed Melbourne and after another General Election, he asked Sir Robert Peel to form a government. Peel could not get the support of the

Irish, so, in February, 1835, the King had to swallow his pride and again ask Melbourne to form a government. With Lord John Russell at the Home Office and Lord Palmerston (reputedly the lover of Melbourne's sister, Emily Cowper) at the Foreign Office, a strong and harmonious cabinet was formed.

Meanwhile, in far-off Australia, two settlements had grown up on the banks of the Yarra river. The Governor, Sir Richard Bourke, with the approval of the King, named one settlement Williamstown, after the King, and the other Melbourne, after his Prime Minister. It is one of the ironies of fate that the Prime Minister's town flourished, whereas the King's town became an insignificant suburb of the great city of Melbourne, Australia.

Lord Melbourne was never short of lady friends and, after the death of his wife, he had found comfort with Emily Eden and then Caroline Norton. When Mrs. Norton decided to separate from her husband, he filed a petition accusing Melbourne of criminal connections with his wife. London revelled in the scandal involving the Prime Minister and rejoiced when George Norton lost his case.

William IV died in June, 1837, and an inexperienced 18-year old girl came to the throne of Great Britain. The Prime Minister, at 58-years old, was full of experience and wisdom, and was looked on almost as a father by the young Queen Victoria. A personal relationship grew up between Melbourne, with his kindly, avuncular charm and the young Victoria, with her eagerness to be educated and instructed by him. She always referred to him as "Dear Lord M." and the London scandal sheets started calling the Queen "Mrs. Melbourne". Victoria was told that one of her Maids-of-Honour, Lady Flora Hastings, was pregnant, and she made Lady Flora submit to a medical examination. Flora was not pregnant as the swelling was caused by a tumour from which she later died. But the enemies of Victoria and Melbourne made the most of this scandal:

"Thus are we ruled by (destiny most wild)
A hungry Premier and a froward child..."

Government was not easy at this time. There was trouble with the Boers in South Africa, and there were rebellions in Canada. Palmerston, at the Foreign Office, was waging wars, mostly of words, on all fronts. At home the Chartists were demanding full adult male suffrage, with which Lord John Russell had to deal. The Melbourne agent, Henry Fox, had died and it was to his nephew, Frederic Francis Fox, that Melbourne wrote on 26th February, 1839: "...in Mansfield and the neighbourhood there is a great deal of arming going on & an intention of rising simultaneously - the same is also said of villages in Leicestershire -

Lord Melbourne, Queen Victoria and Lord Palmerston

I wish you would lose no time in making enquiry as to the foundation which there may be for these alarms..." An Education Bill was passed in this year, together with the proposals for a Penny Post service. But Melbourne's government was surviving on a slender majority and his cabinet was divided. On 7 May, 1839, he handed in his resignation to the Queen and advised her to send for Sir Robert Peel.

Peel laid down a number of conditions which Victoria was unwilling to accept and she implored Melbourne to remain as Prime Minister. He was not very well and he was looking for an easier life, but he agreed to remain in order to please the Queen for whom he still felt a great affection. Although his political will was spent, he soldiered on for another two years in a climate of severe unemployment and a depressed economy The Royal Wedding of the Queen to Prince Albert on 10th February, 1840, was organised by Melbourne and it brought a touch of brightness and glamour to an otherwise drab world. As the Queen's confidence had grown under Melbourne's tutelage, she had gradually taken over the reins of power and Albert now became her chief adviser. In this new Victorian era, Lord Melbourne was seen to be an anachronism: an agnostic, aristocratic, eighteenth-century gentleman who had outlived his age.

The end came in May, 1841, when Melbourne's government was defeated on its Budget proposals. At the ensuing election, Sir Robert Peel was elected with a workable majority. Melbourne resigned and was, perhaps, pleased to give up the burden. Victoria told Peel that she intended to continue to seek the advice of Dear Lord M., though it seems unconstitutional for the Monarch to seek the advice of the Leader of the Opposition. However, Melbourne was a statesman who had inspired her in her youth and had instilled in her the independence and stability of mind which in later years helped her to become the great Queen of her own nation and of an Empire spread around the world.

During his retirement, Lord Melbourne paid regular annual visits to Melbourne Hall, mainly for the autumn shooting. He also maintained his interest in politics as Leader of the Opposition in the House of Lords. Lord Ashley, who had married Melbourne's niece, "Minnie" Cowper, introduced his Mines Act in 1842, which proposed to prohibit the employment of females and boys under the age of 13 in the mines. This affected Melbourne directly, as he owned considerable coal reserves in Greasley and Selston. The mines were leased to Barber, Walker & Co. and after making enquiries, F.F.Fox was able to assure Melbourne that "Women & girls are never employed underground but many boys of all ages are employed...The boys seem very cheerful at their work & grow up of a class to be sober & athletic men..." Fox was also able to supply information about the depressed state of the textile industry. Men had been laid off in Derby and Leicester was in a "terrible state". The reason was that the German and Belgian hosiers' goods were cheaper.

In November, 1842, whilst at Brocket Hall, William suffered a slight stroke. He was visited there by his brother, Frederic, newly married with his young bride, Adine, who immediately set to work to put the house to rights. His sister, Emily, made frequent visits from the Cowper house at Panshanger, not far away. His favourite nephew, William Cowper, was also a frequent visitor. Upon his recovery, Lord Melbourne came to Melbourne Hall and gave Fox detailed instructions: "I will have the room at the end of the passage which is at the left hand of the staircase. There is a dressing room bit in which my servant can stay & so be ready to attend me..." This room is still known as "Lord Melbourne's Room". He had an invitation to Chatsworth where Queen Victoria was staying. However, Victoria had eyes only for her Consort, and Melbourne left Chatsworth a sad and unhappy man.

In his last letter to Fox on 9th November, 1848, Melbourne suggested that Thorney Locusts should be planted in the New Terrace in the gardens at Melbourne Hall. He died suddenly on 26th November, 1848, at Brocket Hall, and was buried quietly in Hatfield church, near his wife Lady Caroline and not in Westminster Abbey as would be expected. A brass plate on a pillar behind the pulpit is his only memorial.

When discussing the life of William Lamb, second Viscount Melbourne, A.J.P.Taylor wrote: "I cannot see that he did much good in his life, apart from contributing to Queen Victoria's political education. On the other hand, I cannot see that he did much harm and that was in itself a considerable achievement". Melbourne's strength and his failing was that he was unbiased and free of dogma and could appreciate both sides of an argument. He could not see how to satisfy both demands simultaneously and therefore, nothing could be done. In his own words, when discussing the peaks and troughs of manufacturing industry, he declared: "This is the nature of things which no human laws can alter though they may perhaps in some respects, modify it".

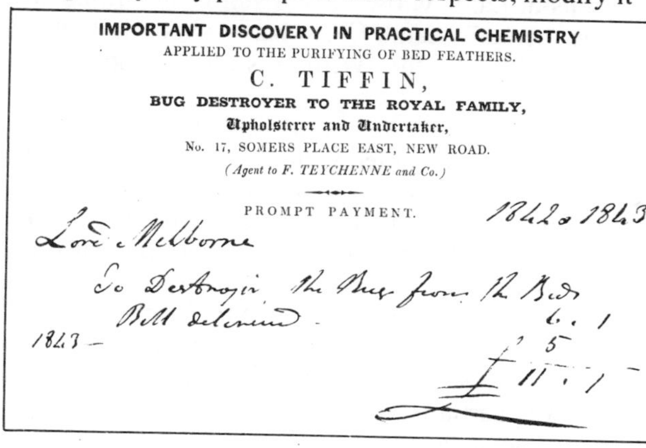
IMPORTANT DISCOVERY IN PRACTICAL CHEMISTRY
APPLIED TO THE PURIFYING OF BED FEATHERS.
C. TIFFIN,
BUG DESTROYER TO THE ROYAL FAMILY,
Upholsterer and Undertaker,
No. 17, SOMERS PLACE EAST, NEW ROAD.
(Agent to F. TEYCHENNE and Co.)
PROMPT PAYMENT.
1842 & 1843
Lord Melborne
To Destroying the Bugs from 12 Beds
Bill delivered 6 . 1
1843 – 5
£11 . 1

Lord Melbourne's bill for destroying bed bugs

Frederic Lamb, 1782-1853. Baron Beauvale, Third Viscount Melbourne.

Frederic Lamb was born in 1782, the third son of Peniston and Elizabeth Lamb. In 1798, he was with William in Glasgow, but he was destined for a life of diplomacy. In 1811, he was appointed to the post of Secretary to the Court of Naples and the Two Sicilies and his father organised a great farewell party. He wrote to Henry Fox at Melbourne: "Mr. Frederic going upon his Embassy has occasion for a great setting out. Can you find anyone that will lend me a Thousand Pounds on my bond?..." His succeeding posts included Vienna, Bavaria and Frankfurt. In 1826, he was Minister Plenipotentiary in Madrid, and the following year he was Ambassador to Portugal. His final post in 1840 was as the British Representative in Vienna.

He was raised to the peerage in 1840 and took his title, Baron Beauvale, from the family estates in Nottinghamshire, having rejected the thought of Baron Haddon or Baron Boothby. On 25 February, 1841, he married in Vienna, the Countess Alexandrine (called Adine for short), the daughter of Count Mahltzann, the Prussian Ambassador at Vienna. Adine was only 24 years old and Frederic was 59. He returned to England in 1842 and went to live at Brocket Hall with brother William. The Lamb family were all captivated by Frederic's young wife, who took over the role of hostess at Brocket, which was badly missing a lady's touch.

On 28th November, 1848, Frederic wrote to Fox informing him of William's death: "Let everything be done at Melbourne as on former occasions. Let all servants at Lamb Close have a suit of mourning each but nothing else be done there..." Lamb Close was a shooting house in Greasley. Frederic inherited his brother William's estates and took the title of third Lord Melbourne.

For the next few years, Fox was bombarded with detailed letters of advice on how to run the estates and improve their profitability, including numerous pamphlets and newspaper articles. Frederic wrote: "...income from rents can create illusion as to the amount of a man's means as it leads inevitably to embarassment and to that I attribute in great part the difficulties which embittered the latter days of My Brother's life..." Frederic reduced his establishment, cut back on repairs and new building and revalued his property. Frederic's tenants at Melbourne objected to the new hard line. Frederic was partially sympathetic: "Indulgences can be given, but arrears cannot be advantageous..."

In 1850, he tried to find a tenant for Melbourne Hall and told Mrs. Holt, the housekeeper, to point out Mrs. Lamb's belongings if a gentleman came to look at the Hall. George Lamb's wife, Caroline, had left Melbourne Hall after George's death but had left her belongings there. The grounds of Melbourne Hall were approved for a fête and the Archaeological Society were allowed to visit the Hall. New evergreens were planted in the gardens and ripe apricots and melons were sent from Melbourne to Brocket by the Northern Railway to Hatfield. Lady Melbourne ordered five pairs of silk muffatees or mittens in bright and nice colours from the Melbourne manufacturers. On 23 September, 1851, Frederic complained: "I can get no drinkable beer brewed in this county. Do you know any good brewer who would come for the job at Brocket Hall and at what price?" Fox moved fast and within a week, Briers was travelling down by rail for the job.

Frederic was suffering severely from gout and he died on 29 January, 1853. In the absence of any male heirs, the title became extinct and the estates passed to Frederic's younger sister, Emily. The young Lady Melbourne was overcome with grief and wrote a pathetic letter to Fox from St. Leonards where she had gone to rest. "My health is much shattered, but they say I shall get better..." Adine did recover, and remarried in 1856 to Lord Forester. She died in 1894 at the age of 77.

Emily Lamb, 1787-1869.
Countess Cowper, Viscountess Palmerston.

The Honourable Emily Mary Lamb was born on 21 April, 1787. She was five years old when the family moved from Piccadilly to the Whitehall house. Her mother's friend, the Duchess of Devonshire, made Emily welcome at Devonshire House, where she would play with the children, who included Caroline St. Jules (later to marry brother, George) and Lady Caroline Ponsonby (later to marry brother, William). In London society, her striking good looks and her kind, sympathetic manner made her in much demand. At the age of 16, she refused Lord Kinnaird's offer of marriage, but she succumbed to the entreaties of Peter Leopold de Grey, fifth Earl Cowper, when she was 18. The wedding at Melbourne House on 20 July, 1805, was a major Whig society event and closely followed brother William's marriage to Caroline Ponsonby.

The newly-weds settled in Earl Cowper's house in Hanover Square, but Emily preferred the country mansion at Panshanger, near Hertford. Emily grew to love this house and used it up to her death. It was only about ten miles from the Lamb house at Brocket Hall. A son and heir was born on 26 June, 1806, christened George Augustus Frederic and took one of his father's subsidiary titles, Lord Fordwich. Emily continued her balls and entertainment at both Hanover Square and Melbourne House, and it was probably at one of these events she became friendly with Henry Temple, third Viscount Palmerston. When a daughter, Emily, was born in 1808, it was thought that Palmerston was the father. To avoid confusion with her mother, Emily was always called "Minnie". A son, William Temple, was born in 1811 and the christian name, Temple, was a tribute to Lord Palmerston. George Spencer was born in 1816 and a daughter, Frances or "Fannie" in 1819.

Almack's Club in King Street, St. James's, was one of the centres of social and political influence. Emily was in charge of the Ladies Committee which decided the guest lists, and ran it with such high standards of perfection, that on one famous occasion, even the Duke of Wellington was excluded because he arrived ten minutes late. Emily was sympathetic to the nervous depression suffered by her sister-in-law, Lady Caroline Lamb and after Caroline had written her scurrilous novel "Glenarvon", Emily sponsored her for membership of Almack's. After Caroline's separation from William in 1825, she became a pathetic figure, and Emily's kind nature overcame all hostility and she paid frequent visits to Brocket to see Caroline up to her death in 1828.

Emily Lamb as a young girl.
The original is at Broadlands, Romsey, Hants.

In 1830, Minnie married Anthony Ashley Cooper, Lord Ashley, the son of the sixth Earl of Shaftesbury. The Lamb family was astonished. Minnie could have had the choice of all the eligible young men about town, but to choose this Evangelical Tory, the son of a penniless peer, went against all their hopes. Emily was happy but brother William and Henry Palmerston thought it a most undesirable match. Palmerston offered Ashley a job in the Foreign Office but it was refused; Ashley couldn't support a Whig administration even though he desperately needed the money. Emily was furious when Wellington refused to support Ashley's election costs and she paid for them herself. Emily's eldest son, George, married Lady Anne Robinson in 1833 and their son Francis, the future seventh Earl Cowper, was born the following year.

Emily's husband, Peter, was a Prince of the Holy Roman Empire, a title bestowed by the Pope in 1778, due to a misdeed of the third Earl. He did not make his mark on the contemporary scene and Emily found rest and contentment with him, perhaps as a respite from the stormy scenes which dominated the Lamb family. He died at the age of 59, in 1837 and Emily was devastated. He was: "...the best of friends and the kindest of husbands. The most benevolent and the kindest of men...I never knew a mortal in whom was less to blame or more to love and admire and respect..." Emily was cheered up when the new Queen Victoria chose Fanny to be a train-bearer at her Coronation in 1838, and her son, William, was elected M.P. for Hertford in 1839.

But, above all, Henry Palmerston continued to pay court to her. They had been great friends all their adult lives, so it was really no surprise when Palmerston proposed marriage. Brothers William and Frederic thought Emily old and wise enough to know her own mind, even if her children did not approve of the marriage of their mother at such an advanced age. The couple were married at St.George's Church, Hanover Square, on

16th December, 1839. It was observed that Emily looked as radiant as a young bride. Her great love for her new husband shines through all her letters; she was a tremendous support to him, without which Palmerston would not have been so successful and popular with the people as he became.

When Lord Melbourne's government fell in 1841, Lord Palmerston held his Tiverton seat, but as he now had no responsibility, Emily persuaded him to take a holiday and visit his Irish estates. On their return, they came straight to Melbourne Hall to spend some time with William. Emily wrote: "...visited Melbourne. The gardens beautiful seen under the worst circumstances (under umbrellas) and it is altogether such a very comfortable place. The six fountains which flow perpetually are seen from so many different vistas that you think the number doubled. The dark walks and yew hedges are also beautiful..." Lord Palmerston was given the post of Foreign Secretary in Lord John Russell's 1846 government and came more and more to dominate Parliament, with the strong support of his wife. William, Lord Melbourne, died at Brocket Hall in 1848. As the family stood around his death bed, Emily was certain that he had gone to heaven, but Lord Ashley had his doubts. Frederic became the third Lord Melbourne and took over the management of the estates. But Frederic was 66 years old and died in 1853. Emily was grief-stricken: "Frederic is gone. I have lost almost the best friend I ever had." All the family estates now passed to Emily as the last survivor of the family of Peniston and Elizabeth Lamb, Lord & Lady Melbourne.

The family visited Melbourne in August, 1853, and Emily wrote: "Really this place is quite lovely and the more I see of it, the more I admire it. I have been round with Fox this morning calling on people of the town and seeing everything; now I have had some lunch and am going out driving with Anne [wife of her son, George]... The weather is very hot and very delicious. We expect Mrs. Lamb [widow of her brother, George] this afternoon..." During this visit, Lord Palmerston laid the foundation stone for the Athenaeum with a silver trowel. The Athenaeum was built on land in Potter Street donated by Emily, and was used as a Mechanics' Institute, Savings Bank and Public Library. The cost of £1200 was raised by public subscription, but Lord and Lady Palmerston were unable to attend the opening ceremony in September, 1854, because of pressure of public affairs.

Emily was now able to use Lord Palmerston's town house in Carlton Gardens as well as his country estate at Broadlands, near Romsey, Hampshire. She also had access to the Lamb houses at Brocket Hall and Melbourne Hall, and her favourite, Panshanger, the Cowper house near Hertford, as well as the de Grey house, Wrest Park in Bedfordshire. She no longer had any use for Melbourne Hall, which had been used only intermittently since her brother, George, had died in 1834. She instructed F.F.Fox to find a suitable tenant for the Hall.

Panshanger from a pencil sketch by Jane Parry in 1825

By 1854, Fox had found tenants, Mr. & Mrs. Brisco, for Melbourne Hall. Brisco made many changes which were approved by Emily. He built a Vinery, cut down some poplars and elm trees in the island and the slip by the water and sold the Melbourne Hall peacocks which kept Mrs.Brisco awake at night. However, when Brisco went bankrupt three years later, he left the Hall in a deplorable state.

The Prime Minister, Lord Aberdeen, declared war on Russia in March, 1854 and sent expeditionary forces to the Crimea. However, the war went disastrously and when Aberdeen resigned, Palmerston was the inevitable and popular choice as Prime Minister. On 12 February, 1855, Fox wrote to "...congratulate your Ladyship on the accession of Lord Palmerston to power as the head of Her Majesty's Government..." Emily's son-in-law, by now Earl Shaftesbury, sent a Sanitary Commission to clean the hospitals at Scutari and Balaclava where Florence Nightingale was struggling against red tape and the insanitary conditions which were prevalent there. The military situation improved and on 10 September, 1855, Emily wrote: "...This great news of the taking of Sevastopol which we have just heard is the cause of this change as there must be a Cabinet Wednesday to settle many things. When the Malakoff Tower was taken the Russians evacuated the town, burning their vessels & blowing up their magazines..."

The Crimean War dragged on into the New Year, but on 22 March, 1856, Emily was able to write: "...We shall certainly have peace very soon declared, but I don't think we shall get back the American market..." Fox wanted to organise celebrations in Melbourne to commemorate the end of the Crimean War and Emily suggested Tea, a Procession and Fireworks or some kind of music, towards which she subscribed £10. The rejoicings were tinged with sadness at the death of her eldest son, George, sixth Earl Cowper at the early age of 50. Her grandson, Francis, became the seventh Earl.

With the boom in heavy industry, coal and iron were in great demand, and Emily saw this as a means of increasing the income from the estates. The Nottinghamshire estates were developing their coal reserves rapidly, and the discovery of ironstone at Selston gave hopes of further success, but it was of low quality. The ironstone at Duston in Northamptonshire was more successful and Mr. Pell developed these deposits with great vigour. However, he had a habit of not paying his rents and royalties and when he went bankrupt in 1865, Emily refused to go to law with Pell as "...we owe him a great deal for his Spirit and Enterprize and his Activity which has brought Duston ore to the high Character it now enjoys..."

Lord & Lady Palmerston attempted to pay annual visits to Melbourne, but these frequently had to be cancelled. On 12 August, 1855, Emily wrote: "We have settled to start by the 10.30 Train as it is better to have one Carriage, and this gives one a little more time as we must be at the Station a half of an hour before Railway time to get the Carriage put on. Pray order a pair of horses to be at Kegworth at 2.50..." However, this visit was cancelled as the Queen was in Paris and Palmerston was engaged with the Crimean War. They had intended to visit the new colliery at Greasley and the Nottinghamshire tenants had prepared a tremendous welcome for the pair, which had to be cancelled.

The 1857 election was the first test of Palmerston's popularity as Prime Minister. Emily instructed Fox to raise support for him in her estates and particularly in Duston where Lord Althorpe was not considered a good candidate. On 5 April, 1857, she wrote: "...glad that most of the Elections went off so well. Lord Althorpe was particularly gratifying... And the Elections all over the Country have gone wonderfully in Lord Palmerston's favour. Our reception at Tiverton & Torquay and all along that road was quite Enthusiastic - people waiting at all the Stations to cheer us and to shake hands with Lord P..." The proposed visit to Melbourne in 1857 had to be cancelled due to parliamentary business with the Indian Mutiny and they could only visit Broadlands where they were close to a railway Telegraph.

Palmerston's government was defeated in February, 1858, on a Conspiracy bill and the Earl of Derby led a Conservative administration with young Benjamin Disraeli as Home Secretary. However, the election in the following year gave Palmerston the majority of seats and he formed a new administration with Lord John Russell as Foreign Secretary and William Gladstone as Chancellor of the Exchequer. This government marks the transition of the old Whig party to the modern Liberal party. Emily wrote: "...in general all people have behaved well...for the purpose of forming a strong Government, at a time when it seemed most necessary for the public good..." The 1859 visit to Melbourne was cancelled "...as Lord Palmerston has so much business that he has not yet been able to leave London...The idle workmen who are now striking for nine hours work instead of ten are little aware of this labour of being Prime Minister and having occupation all day and half the night besides..."

The Palmerstons were not able to visit Melbourne in 1860 as Emily caught a severe cold on her husband's tour of Leeds and Rotherham. They had intended to attend the opening ceremony for the restoration of Melbourne church, for which Emily had donated £20 for the bazaar and had given 2,000 feet of stone without charge. There was no visit in 1861 as Lord Palmerston was installed as Warden of the Cinque Ports: "...Lord Palmerston's installation at Dover was a splendid sight and most gratifying to him in every way. The Queen herself could not have been received with more enthusiasm. The Town was cover'd with Flags & Banners & triumphal arches..." This gave Emily another country house, Walmer Castle, at which she could stay. In December of that year, Prince Albert died of typhoid and the Queen went into deep mourning. Emily wrote: "...I am glad to say that Lord Palmerston has thrown off his gout entirely and is nearly as well as usual, walking about without Crutch or Stick...The Queen's health is wonderfully good considering the overwhelming affliction she has suffered..."

They squeezed in a visit to Melbourne in September, 1862, and the "Derby Reporter" noted that, at a lunch, the inhabitants "welcomed Lord Palmerston again to the neighbourhood with something, perhaps, of the undertone of a partially neglected tenantry, enumerated his acts of wisdom, and firmly though mildly touched upon his faults..." His policy of non-intervention in the American Civil War was approved. The Palmerstons also visited Over Haddon and Nottinghamshire. However, Emily was now 75 years old and Palmerston was 77, and although both were very fit, this was their last visit to Melbourne. Emily continued her strong guidance to Fox on the running of the Estates and took a great interest in what was going on. There was a severe water shortage in 1864 and an outbreak of foot-and-mouth disease in 1865.

In September, 1865, the couple went to Brocket Hall for a rest. Emily wrote: "...Lord Palmerston & myself are still here, the quiet & the bracing air of this place have done his health so much good, and I have no doubt he will be quite well again before the winter..." Later, Lord Palmerston caught a chill when out riding; he was thought to be improving when he had a mutton chop and a glass of port for breakfast, but he died on the 18th October, surrounded by the three women he loved most, Emily, Minnie and Fanny. Here, at Brocket Hall, Emily had seen her two brothers, William and Frederic die. She had survived all her brothers, her two husbands, her eldest son and her son-in-law and a number of her grandchildren, but other children were around to console her in her loss. Palmerston was buried with due ceremony in the "Statesman's Aisle", the North Transept of Westminster Abbey on 28th October, 1865.

Emily was overwhelmed with grief and it was two months before she was able to restart her correspondence with her Melbourne agent. "...I have been able to answer very few of the shoals of letters I received every day. The public Addresses I had from Corporations were answered by Mr. Evelyn Ashley for me and amounted to nearly three Hundred! There never was such sincere regrets & sorrow as has been evinced all over the world and people have shewn their good feelings in every way and it is certainly very gratifying to my heart to see him so regretted and so appreciated every where, but I, who look only now to peace & quiet and a retired life feel it often very irksome to receive such a number of letters.." She gave up the Palmerston home, Cambridge House, Piccadilly, and moved to 21, Park Lane. "...It is a fine and healthy situation looking over the Park and I shall be as comfortable there as I can be after suffering such an irreparable and overwhelming loss and all my happiness on Earth..."

Lady Palmerston continued her interest in Estate management and advised Fox on getting rid of the weeds on Melbourne Pool, but she was not enamoured with Fox's complicated scheme for rearranging the farms at Melbourne. She wished to avoid unnecessary expense as she was the last of the Entail of Lord Melbourne's Marriage Settlement and wanted to pass a prosperous estate on to her grandson. She approved subscriptions to the Miners' Hospital at Eastwood, the Chancel roof at Duston, the Congregational chapel at Greasley and a school at Bagthorpe.

Politics still interested her and she objected to Lord Derby's government of 1866 with Disraeli as Home Secretary. "...This country is certainly in a very dangerous position with this horrid reform bill!!...D'Israeli has no principles of any Sort and no stake in the Country..." In 1868, when Disraeli became Prime Minister, she wrote: "...We are all dreadfully disgusted at the prospect of having a Jew for our prime minister..." At the 1868 election, Emily, now 81 years old, was down in Romsey, fighting for the Liberals. Her son, William Cowper, was elected and she was thrilled by the occasion: "...It was a hard fought Battle and my presence here had an Immense effect in carrying the day and reviving all the old recollections of Lord Palmerston and I was immensely cheer'd as I drove about with my Old Grey Horses..."

She approved the sale of a piece of land in High Street for the Melbourne Congregational Church, and gave in to Fox when he wanted to buy property in Castle Street. Colonel Gooch, the tenant at Melbourne Hall, had died and his widow, Mrs. Gooch, invited Emily to visit her. "...I have so much to do here [Brocket] and in Hampshire that I am afraid I shall not be able to accept Mrs. Gooch's kind invitation, but I will write and thank her. If I felt up to such a Journey it would have given me great pleasure to see Melbourne again with all its improvements..."

This was her last letter to Melbourne and two weeks later, on 11th September, 1869, this grand old lady died. In her lifetime, she had seen the world change from the exotic lives of the eighteenth-century Whig aristocrats to the sterner morals of Victorian rectitude and she had changed with it. Her son-in-law, Lord Shaftesbury, wrote of her "...unceasing thoughts and acts of kindness, generosity and affection. Poor, dear, beloved Mum, it is a very terrible thing to have lost her..." She was buried in Westminster Abbey beside her second husband.

Francis de Grey, K.G, 1834-1905. Seventh Earl Cowper.

Francis Thomas de Grey was born in 1834, the eldest son of George, sixth Earl Cowper and Anne Florence, his wife. Francis was granted the customary title of the eldest son, Lord Fordwich. He was educated at Harrow and Christ Church, Oxford, from which he graduated with a Master's degree. On the death of his father in 1856, he inherited the titles of seventh Earl Cowper, eighth Baron Butler and tenth Baron Dingwall. He also received the inherited honour of Prince of the Holy Roman Empire as well as his father's estates in Kent, Hertfordshire and Yorkshire and the houses at Panshanger, Ratling Court and Wrest Park. He succeeded his mother as seventh Baron Lucas upon her death in 1880. He was created a Knight of the Garter and was a Privy Councillor.

When his grandmother, Emily, Lady Palmerston, died in 1869, he also received the Lamb family estates of Melbourne and Brocket Hall. In 1870, he married Katrine Compton, the niece of the Marquess of Northampton. To celebrate the event, F.F.Fox arranged entertainments on the Melbourne estates. The earl instructed Fox: "...not to be sparing of any reasonable expense. If you err at all it will be better to err on the side of too great liberality..." Fox gave 140 Melbourne tenants a large dinner, their wives and families had a substantial tea at the Athenaeum with a good band and dancing for 350 people, a treat for the National School children and meat for the poorer inhabitants. Similar treats were arranged for the Nottinghamshire tenants, costing £450 and the festivities at Over Haddon cost £50. Earl Cowper was taken aback at the cost: "the expense is a great deal...the whole thing seems to have been very much appreciated and perhaps it was as well to be on the safe side..."

Francis was a keen sportsman and spent much of his holidays shooting in Scotland at Glenmoriston or on the Isle of Mull. The shooting at Melbourne was leased out, but High Park Wood in Nottinghamshire promised good sport. He decided to build himself a new house in the woods here, which he could use as a shooting lodge. The house was called Beauvale House and was designed by Edward Godwin of Regents Park, London. It had a high central observation tower, from which there was a good view of the surrounding woodlands. Local labour and materials were used for the construction and the garden shrubs were supplied by James Smith of Darley Dale. Earl Cowper had several arguments with Godwin, who did not obey his instructions: "...[Mr.Godwin] has already annoyed me very much by having all the internal woodwork painted after we had particularly settled that it was to be merely varnished...You might ask the builder at Beauvale whether it is too late to scrape the paint off the woodwork of our bedroom and the staircases..." Fox agreed to strip the paint off but thought it not worth changing the paint in the attics. The first shoot was held in 1874.

Beauvale House.
Sketch by Jack Bronson,
Eastwood.

Earl Cowper made a survey of his estates which were managed from Melbourne. These included Greasley and Selston, Boothby Graffoe, Melton Mowbray, Over Haddon and Duston. All the estates had been entailed in Peniston Lamb's Marriage Settlement of 1769, and the Earl was the first inheritor free of the Entail and was able to dispose of them as he wished. In order to tidy up the straggling estate, he sold Melton Mowbray and Sysonby in May, 1870, for £41,312 and Boothby Graffoe in August, 1871, for £79,140. The Nottinghamshire estates were too valuable to sell.

Francis was as free with his donations as his grandmother, particularly for helping churches and schools. He gave £20 to the Wesleyan Chapel and £30 and stone to the Congregational church in Melbourne. He assisted the Free church at Ironville, Hill Top church, Portland Row chapel, Jacksdale chapel, Greasley parish church and new churches at Westwood and Underwood, all in Nottinghamshire. He helped with the restoration of Duston parish church and donated the site for a new church at Over Haddon in 1879. The Athenaeum and schools in Melbourne as well as schools in Kimberley, Beauvale and Underwood were subjects of his generosity. During the 1870's, there were several hard winters and the earl subscribed to the soup and coal funds, and set unemployed men cleaning out the ponds at the Moats in Melbourne

The Enclosure of Selston Common in Nottinghamshire in 1877 caused rifts between Earl Cowper and his tenants. One of the objectors, Mr. De Morgan organised meetings to protest against the enclosure and received widespread support. There were riots on Selston Common when the enclosure fences were erected and the fences were broken down. The ringleaders were brought before the Courts, accused of trespass, and the whole sorry affair dragged on for several years. Earl Cowper had some sympathy for the cottagers who had paid very low rents for their cottages erected upon the waste and were now called upon to pay large rents. He was also unhappy with Fox's performance in the affair and threatened to sack Fox for writing to the Enclosure Commissioners without permission.

In 1880, Earl Cowper was appointed Lord-Lieutenant of Ireland and took up residence in Dublin Castle. He nominated his brother, Henry, to run the estates in his absence. However, Henry was unable to make decisions, which always had to be referred back to Earl Cowper in Dublin. It was an unfortunate time in Ireland The political demand for Home Rule was powerful and Parnell was imprisoned for obstructing the work of the House of Commons. In addition, Countess Cowper had a narrow escape from an accident in a phaeton and pair of ponies, near Dublin Castle. It was this that caused Francis to hand in his resignation and he returned to England in 1882. The Melbourne agent, Frederic Francis Fox died on 24 March, 1883. He had served both the second and third Lords Melbourne, Lady Palmerston and Earl Cowper and was succeeded by his assistant, William Garratt.

In 1875, Melbourne Hall was let to Mr. William Dashwood Fane, a retired barrister, for £200 a year. Fane became an important member of Melbourne society, he was a pillar of the church and organised the celebrations for Queen Victoria's Golden Jubilee in 1887. With Earl Cowper's approval, he spent long periods sorting out the Melbourne Hall documents, stored in the Muniment Room. Eventually, a number of these were published in three volumes by The Historic Manuscripts Commission. When his cousin, Henry Fane, of Fulbeck Hall in Lincolnshire went bankrupt, he bought Fulbeck and left Melbourne to live there in 1894.

Earl Cowper's nephew, Auberon Herbert, had controlled the shooting in Beauvale, but when the Boer War broke out, Herbert went to South Africa in 1900, with Buller, as the "Times" correspondent. The shooting was therefore done by neighbours until Herbert returned.

Francis, Earl Cowper died in July, 1905 and was buried in Hertingfordbury church with his ancestors. An article in "Country Life" for July, 1904, had described him as "...one of the most beloved and universally respected of all the great landlords of England..." At the time of his death, he was landlord to 43,000 acres of land, one town and five country houses, each with their own supporting estates, which were valued for probate at £1,179,714. There were no children of his marriage and no other surviving male heirs, therefore the Cowper title became extinct. The estates were broken up and divided between his widow, his nephew, Auberon Herbert, his niece, Lady Desborough, and his sister, Lady Amabel Kerr. Lady Amabel received Melbourne Hall and Brocket Hall with their estates, but the Nottinghamshire property was put into Trust for his widow and later sold to pay death duties.

Lady Amabel Cowper
from a mirror in
Melbourne Hall.

The Kerrs of Melbourne

Lady Amabel Cowper was born in 1846, daughter of the sixth Earl Cowper and his wife, Anne Florence, and sister to the seventh Earl. She was affectionately known to her family as Amy and spent much of her childhood in her mother's home at Wrest Park. She was converted to Catholicism, following a long Protestant family history. She was an accomplished author and her books were mainly on Catholic subjects. In 1873, she married Lord Walter Talbot Kerr, the fourth son of the seventh Marquis of Lothian and a Captain in the Royal Navy. The wedding was a Catholic ceremony in Arundel Cathedral. Anne Florence was taken with her new son-in-law and wrote: "I am so very much amused at your coming back to your first love, Portsmouth Harbour, only you have changed Captain Kerr versus Hastings..." In another letter she wrote: "...I can't say how happy I am you have got such a frisky husband. It will be the making of you..."

Lord Walter Kerr was born in 1839 and joined the Royal Navy as a young midshipman in 1853. He was a member of Sir William Peel's Naval Brigade in the Indian Mutiny of 1857-8 and was present at the Reliefs of Cawnpore and Lucknow. He was captain of H.M.S. Agincourt at the time of his marriage to Lady Amabel and a few years later commanded H.M.S. Minotaur. In 1887-8, he was appointed Aide-de-Camp to Queen Victoria and then became Commander-in-Chief of the Channel Fleet on board H.M.S. Trafalgar, with the rank of Admiral of the Fleet. In 1899, he took up the task of Senior Naval Lord. His decorations included the Grand Cross of the Order of the Bath and Grand Cross of the Order of St. George, but possibly his greatest decoration was the Humane Society Silver Medal for rescuing a sailor from the River Tagus in Portugal.

A son, Ralph Francis, was born in 1874. After taking an honours degree at Oxford, he was called to Holy Orders and became an Oratorian priest and finally a Priest Superior at the Brompton Oratory in London. Ralph gave up all claims to his inheritance. A second son, Andrew William, was born in 1881, followed by two more sons, Philip and John and two daughters, Margaret and Mary. Mary later became a nun. In 1894, Lady Amabel's cousin, Lord Ripon, left to her the church and property of St. Damiano in Assisi. The chapel was built by St. Francis and, in 1215, St. Clare, who founded the nuns of the Franciscan order, lived there. These nuns were known in England as the "Poor Clares" because of their vows of poverty. In 1896, Lady Amabel built a Catholic church and presbytery in her brother's Nottinghamshire estates at Hill Top, Eastwood.

In 1905 when the seventh Earl Cowper died, Melbourne Hall with its property at Over Haddon and Duston, as well as Brocket Hall with property in Hatfield, Welwyn, Wheathampstead and Ayot St. Peter was left to Lady Amabel. At this time, Lady Amabel and Lord Walter were staying with the Throckmortons, at Coughton Court. They owned a town house in South Kensington, but resolved to take up permanent residence at Melbourne Hall. The move took place in January, 1906, but Lady Amabel did not live long to enjoy her new home and she died in October, 1906.

Lord Walter decided to build a Catholic church in Melbourne, in memory of his wife. He employed Evans & Son of Nottingham as Architects; they had designed Lady Amabel's church at Hill Top, Eastwood. The foundation stone was laid by the Bishop of Nottingham on 19 July, 1907 and the church was open for services by 1909.. It cost £2430 and the accompanying Presbytery house £650, and they were financed and maintained by the owners of Melbourne Hall. The church and presbytery at Hill Top were conveyed to the Bishop of Nottingham. After Lord Walter's death, his banner, which had hung in the Chapel of the Order of the Bath, was hung in Melbourne Catholic church.

Lord Walter was too old to serve in the 1914-1918 War, but he followed the careers of his sons with interest and pride. Andrew was a Captain in the Navy, Philip served in South Africa and John was a Captain in the Army, initially guarding the East Coast. Later, in the trenches, John narrowly escaped severe wounding by shelling. Lord Walter did not believe the rumours of the Battle of Jutland in 1916: "...I fear that I doubt the truth of the yarn about the Grand Fleet having done something big - As a matter of fact by doing what they are all this time - is doing more for the Allies than if they won another Trafalgar - Keeping the Germans bottled up..." Estate workmen were called up for service and Lord Walter complained when he found that his Super Tax demand was nearly as much as his Rental income. In 1919, the War Office allotted Lord Walter a damaged German machine gun with ammunition box and accessories, as a trophy of the War.

He continued to live at Melbourne Hall, but was faced with the payment of death duties on the estates of, not only his wife, but also her brother, Francis, who had died 15 months earlier. He found himself obliged to sell some of his property and decided to sell the Duston estate of 1045 acres together with five farms and "The Melbourne Arms" public house in 1919. Outlying portions of the Brocket estate including Wheathampstead Place were offered for sale by auction in 1919. The carved fireplace overmantel in the dining room at Melbourne Hall was brought by Lord Walter from Wheathampstead Place Farm. The sale of Brocket Hall itself, with its 573 acre Park and its collections of furniture and pictures and its library of 5000 books followed in 1923. The Estate Agent thought it best to sell quickly as the development of Welwyn Garden City did not seem advantageous. The Cavendish Bridge property in Castle Donington was sold in 1922, leaving the Melbourne Estate consisting only of property in Melbourne and Over Haddon.

Following an accident to his leg, Father Ralph came to live at Melbourne for over a year while recuperating. Lord Walter spent the winters in London and the summers in Melbourne. He devoted himself to improving the Hall and decided to add on the Billiard Room in 1911, installing telephones and a wireless for Ralph's benefit, and having the house completely electrically rewired He also tidied up and restored the Gardens which had been much neglected. He retained an interest in his remaining property in Melbourne and Over Haddon until his death, at the age of 88, in 1927. He was buried in the Lothian family vault in the Catholic Church at Dalkeith.

Andrew Kerr was born 23 March, 1881. He followed his father's naval career and served in the First World War, He was Captain of H.M.S. Cawnpore in Captain Sturdee's naval action in the Falkland Islands in December, 1914, but his ship was unable to keep up with the fleet during the pursuit of Admiral Von Spee. He served during the Battle of Jutland and was also involved in the Gallipoli Expedition. In 1915, he married his third cousin, Marie Constance, only daughter of Walter Raleigh Kerr, at the Brompton Oratory. They had two sons, Peter, born in 1922, and John, born in 1927. He was fonder of Melbourne than any of his predecessors and wrote: "I think we need not fear anything as regards the Melbourne Estate going bankrupt, which is a blessing because I was and am still if necessary prepared to sell my last pair of boots to keep it going..." Andrew and Marie divided their time between their house in London and a summer residence, "Minnehaha" at Ferring-on-Sea, Sussex, but eventually lived mainly at Melbourne. Marie commented that Ferring was "full of horrid little houses; however the Prince of Wales was here last week and so no doubt it will now become fashionable..."

Andrew and Marie were living permanently in Melbourne Hall in 1928, but Andrew died suddenly in 1929. Marie continued to live at Melbourne and her children were brought up here. She converted Andrew's bedroom into a Chapel and decorated it with the Stations of the Cross, a painting of c.1360 by Lippo Memmi and family memorabilia. She became a popular and well-loved figure in the town, and was a great supporter of the Red Cross Society. In 1935, land at Cockshut Lane was donated to Melbourne as a playing field in memory of Lord Walter and Captain Andrew Kerr. When Marie Kerr died in 1980 at the great age of 92, Rosemary Meynell wrote: "We all mourn her loss. A great light has gone out in Derbyshire." Both Andrew and Marie were buried at Dalkeith.

Peter Kerr was educated at Ampleforth College, York and Christchurch College, Oxford. In 1940, Philip, the eleventh Marquis of Lothian, died in the U.S.A. where he was British Ambassador. The title of twelfth Marquis of Lothian passed to his 18-year old second cousin, Peter. In his will, Philip had left the Lothian house and estate at Blickling Hall to the National Trust, with which he had been closely associated. This was the first endowed stately home to be received by the National Trust. The Lothian estate in the Scottish borders around Jedburgh with its mansion of Monteviot was inherited by Peter Kerr, the new Lord Lothian.

Peter married Antonella Newland in 1943 when he was serving in the Scots Guards in the war. They had two sons, Michael and Ralph, and four daughters, Mary, Cecil, Clare and Elizabeth. The eldest son, Michael took his father's courtesy title of Earl of Ancram. Lord Lothian undertook political service with the United Nations and the European Parliament. He was Parliamentary Private Secretary to the Foreign Secretary, Lord Home, from 1960-1963 and was twice a Lord-in-Waiting (Government Whip) in the House of Lords. He was Parliamentary Under-Secretary to the Minister of Health in 1964 and and Under-Secretary of State at the Foreign Office in 1970. He chaired the Scottish Council of the Red Cross Society from 1976-1986 and was appointed to the post of Lord Warden of the Stannaries for the Duchy of Cornwall from 1977-1983.

His wife is a journalist, and worked as current affairs columnist for the Scottish Daily Express from 1966-1970. She is a Fellow of the Institute of Journalists. She is renowned for her institution of the "Woman of the Year Lunch" to which invitations are limited to professional women who have made a significant mark in national and community affairs. She chaired the Order of Christian Unity and won the Templeton UK Award in 1992 for " a significant contribution to the field of spiritual values". She is currently working on a biography of Valentina Tereshkova, the Russian cosmonaut and the first woman in space. She was responsible for the idea of opening Melbourne Hall and Gardens to the public, and opened a teashop and gift shop in the outbuildings of Melbourne Hall.

Lord and Lady Lothian purchased Ferniehurst Castle, near Jedburgh, from the Lothian Trust, and restored it as a family home. Monteviot and the Jedburgh Estates were made over to their eldest son, Michael. They wished to transfer Melbourne Hall to their youngest son, Ralph. However, Melbourne Hall was not a viable proposition as there was little income to support it. The remaining farms at Over Haddon had been sold in the 1950's, and much property in Melbourne had been sold in the

1970's in an attempt to maintain the building. The future of the Hall looked bleak but Lord and Lady Lothian determined to save the Hall and in 1988, two Trust Funds were set up, one for the Hall and one for the Gardens. These funds were financed by the sale of substantial pieces of land. They also sold documents of national interest from the famous Melbourne Muniments to the British Library. When Sir John Coke and Thomas Coke stored their papers at Melbourne, they could not have realised that at some time in the future, these papers would save the Hall for their descendants. The Catholic chapel at Melbourne was conveyed to the Bishop of Nottingham and St. Damiano was returned to the world wide Order of Franciscan Friars.

On the occasion of the bicentenary of the "First Fleet" which sailed to Australia in 1788, Lord and Lady Lothian wished to commemorate the event to further cement the links with Melbourne, Australia. In keeping with the ambience of the Gardens, it was decided to commission a lead urn in the manner of the John Nost urns which had been standing in the Gardens for 280 years. The urn was unveiled by the Agent-General for Victoria on 24th September, 1988. It was crafted by John Lennox, the sculptor, of Leamington Spa.

From left to right The Lord Lieutenant of Derbyshire, Peter Hilton; Agent-General, Ian Haig and Lord Lothian.

Unveiling of the Bicentenary Urn in 1988.

In 1988, Lord Ralph Kerr married Marie-Claire Black at St. Andrews Cathedral in Fife and took up residence at Melbourne Hall. The Trusts had been set up successfully, with some support from English Heritage. Lord and Lady Ralph have three sons, John, James and Francis, and the

Hall is now a family home again, the cries of children echoing through the rooms. Lord Ralph is the Derbyshire representative for Sothebys and he is a pianist and composer. Lady Ralph is a portrait painter of some renown. Melbourne Hall has been owned by civil servants, public servants, statesmen and stateswomen, soldiers and sailors, as well as dilettantes. It is now owned by a young, artistic family who intend to continue to look after their 365-year old inheritance.

SELECT BIBLIOGRAPHY

Young, Michael — "Servility & Service: The Life and Work of Sir John Coke". (Royal Historical Society, 1986)

Dunckley, Henry — "Lord Melbourne". (1892)

Cecil, David — "The Young Melbourne". (Constable, 1939)
"Lord M.". (Constable, 1954)

Ziegler, Philip — "Melbourne". (Collins, 1976)

Jenkins, Elizabeth — "Lady Caroline Lamb". (1932)

Airlie, Countess of — "Lady Palmerston and her Times". (1922)

Lever, Tresham — "The Letters of Lady Palmerston". (1957)

Rodley, Jasper — "Lord Palmerston". (Constable, 1970)

Pollock, John — "Shaftesbury: The Poor Man's Earl". (Hodder & Stoughton, 1985)

THE OWNERS OF MELBOURNE HALL 1628 to 1993

1) Marie Powell = SIR JOHN COKE = 2) Joan Lee
1563 - 1644

SIR JOHN COKE THE YOUNGER = Elizabeth Pusey
1607 - 1650

THOMAS COKE = Mary Pope
d. 1656 | d. 1656

COLONEL JOHN COKE = Mary Leventhorpe
1653 - 1692 | d. 1681

1) Lady Mary Stanhope = VICE - CHAMBERLAIN THOMAS COKE = 2) Mary Hale
d. 1704 | 1674 - 1727

John d. 1739 | Elizabeth (Betsy) 1676 - 1739 | Mary | Alice d. 1758 | Dorothy b. & d. 1679 | Francis b. & d. 1680

Mary | Elizabeth

GEORGE LEWIS COKE 1715 - 1750 | Charlotte Coke BORN 1719 = MATTHEW LAMB created Bart. 1755 died 1768 | Anna Maria Coke born 1713

Charlotte d. 1790

PENISTON, 1st LORD MELBOURNE = Elizabeth Milbanke
1748 - 1828 | 1752 - 1818

Peniston 1770 - 1805

Lady Caroline Ponsonby = WILLIAM, 2nd LORD MELBOURNE
1785 - 1828 | 1779 - 1848

FREDERICK 3rd LORD MELBOURNE 1782 - 1853

George 1784 - 1834

1) 5th Earl Cowper = EMILY = 2) HENRY TEMPLE 2nd LORD PALMERSTON
d. 1837 | 1787 - 1869 | 1784 - 1865

Harriet 1789 - 1803

Augustus 1807 - 1836

Lady Anne de Grey, Baroness Lucas = GEORGE 6th EARL COWPER

ADMIRAL OF THE FLEET LORD WALTER KERR d. 1927 = LADY AMABEL COWPER d. 1906

7th EARL COWPER d. 1905

Fr. Ralph Kerr (Oratorian Priest)

CAPTAIN ANDREW KERR = Marie Constance Kerr
d. 1929 | d. 1980

Mary (entered religious life) | Margaret (Spinster) | John = Amabel Ward | Philip = Dorothy Cave

PETER, 12th MARQUESS OF LOTHIAN = Antonella Newland
born 1922

Lord John Kerr = Isabel Gurney
born 1927

Lady Mary Kerr = Charles von Westenholtz | Michael Kerr, Earl of Ancram = Lady Jane Fitzalan Howard | Lady Cecil Kerr = Donald Cameron of Lochiel | Lady Clare Kerr = James FitzRoy, Earl of Euston | Lady Elizabeth Kerr = Richard Montagu Douglas Scott, Earl of Dalkeith | LORD RALPH KERR = Marie Claire Black John Frederic Francis

William Kerr | David Kerr | Andrew Kerr | Marion Kerr | Catherine Kerr